Synthesis Lectures on Information Concepts, Retrieval, and Services

Series Editor

Gary Marchionini, School of Information and Library Science, The University of North Carolina at Chapel Hill, Chapel Hill, NC, USA

This series publishes short books on topics pertaining to information science and applications of technology to information discovery, production, distribution, and management. Potential topics include: data models, indexing theory and algorithms, classification, information architecture, information economics, privacy and identity, scholarly communication, bibliometrics and webometrics, personal information management, human information behavior, digital libraries, archives and preservation, cultural informatics, information retrieval evaluation, data fusion, relevance feedback, recommendation systems, question answering, natural language processing for retrieval, text summarization, multimedia retrieval, multilingual retrieval, and exploratory search.

Wei Ding · Xia Lin · Michael Zarro

Information Architecture and UX Design

The Integration of Information Spaces

Third Edition

 Springer

Wei Ding
Consumer Financial Protection Bureau
Washington, DC, USA

Xia Lin
Drexel University
Philadelphia, PA, USA

Michael Zarro
Phenom
Ambler, PA, USA

ISSN 1947-945X   ISSN 1947-9468 (electronic)
Synthesis Lectures on Information Concepts, Retrieval, and Services
ISBN 978-3-031-72137-3   ISBN 978-3-031-72138-0 (eBook)
https://doi.org/10.1007/978-3-031-72138-0

Preface

The term Information Architecture (IA) was coined by a brick-and-mortar architect Richard Wurman in the early 1970s as a profession of "gathering, organizing, and presenting information." The World Wide Web accelerated the information explosion and created the real needs for the profession to help more people find and manage useful information online. Similarly, User Experience (UX), a term first used by Don Norman at Apple Computer in the 1990s, grew exponentially along with the web.

Our revised third edition positions IA and UX design are two sides of the same human-centered design (HCD) coin. IA is associated with taxonomy, metadata, thesaurus, and other "information findability" related tasks that often happen behind the scenes, along with labeling and defining channels for information access. UX design is responsible for the vision and design solutions that people interact with and experience.

The authors believe that the continuous evolution of the information spaces supported by the web, cloud, and Artificial Intelligence (AI) technologies makes it possible to deliver ever more sophisticated interactions and user activities. The increasing importance of large language models (LLMs) and Generative AI (GenAI) have had profound impacts on work, play, and society at large. UX and AI converge in human-centered AI (HCAI), with the responsibility to make AI work for people. This requires a team effort including data scientists, machine learning engineers, developers, product owners, graphic designers, user researchers, and many more.

Convergence calls for higher level of seamless collaboration among all the disciplines, but it does not eliminate the need for dedicated IA and UX work. Instead, this work spreads from traditional web design to digital devices, apps, medical devices, automobiles, and many other places. IAs and UX designers are part of the team determining the business and UX strategy, based on user needs and business goals, and making sure the strategy gets carried out.

Drawing on the authors' extensive experience as practitioners, HCI researchers, and IA instructors, this book outlines a balanced view of the UX discipline by connecting practitioner's real-world experience and IA/UX practices to human information behavioral theories, design principles, and guidelines. In addition to demonstrating conventional IA deliverables, techniques, and tools, this book emphasizes that IA is about the design and integration of information spaces (both digital and physical) beyond the Web. This expansion requires new skillsets like Design Thinking and Systems Thinking, to analyze and design highly interconnected systems that exponentially increase the benefits to the people in them.

Uses of the Book

This book is a result of our teaching of a graduate-level course on Information Architecture at Drexel University for many years. The content has been constantly updated to incorporate the latest developments in the field—including GenAI and Systems Thinking for this third edition. The objective of the course was to introduce fundamental IA/UX concepts, theories, processes, and techniques in the context of human-centered design, to graduate students majored in Information Sciences and Information Systems. As the book was originally written as lecture notes, we believe it is most suitable to be used as textbook for similar courses in other schools. The key features of the book include concise discussions structured around each topic and the balanced coverage of theoretical and practical issues. As Drexel's courses are quarter courses typically include 10 lecture weeks, we have conveniently structured the book into ten chapters, one for each week. The content for each week can be easily expanded when used for a semester course.

User experience practitioners should also find this book useful and inspiring as a starting point in their exploration of this exciting field. We hope this book can help bridge the gap between the community of practice and academia.

Structure of the Book

The book covers the following topics:

- **Information Architecture and UX Design: Definition and Evolution**: Chapter 1 discusses the definition of Information Architecture and UX in the context of integrated information spaces, its impact on the way people interact with information, and relationships to other disciplines. Chapter 2 takes a historical perspective to examine the evolution of the web and beyond, and identifies new challenges and opportunities for UX in the context of a generative generation marked by rapid development of GenAI.

- **Human-Centered Design methods and principles**: Chapter 3 introduces the Human-Centered Design methodology, which is the prerequisite for conducting any IA/UX practices. As the core of the book, Chaps. 4–7 are dedicated to the IA key concepts and foundations including information organization and navigation, human information behavior, and the corresponding design implications, as well as interaction design patterns, principles, and best practices. These chapters incorporate the latest developments in the field like AI for user research, and reflect the current state of knowledge for usability researchers and user experience design professionals.
- **Design Thinking and Systems Thinking**: This new Chap. 8 compares Design Thinking and Systems Thinking, two important approaches for integrating information spaces. We share the zoom-in/zoom-out approach, examining systems from a high level in Systems Thinking to find leverage points where and intervention may have a substantial impact, and the more detailed approach in Design Thinking to craft human-centered solutions that are also viable for the business.
- **IA in Practice**: In Chap. 9, the design and development team is discussed. Frameworks like Agile development and Lean UX are related to the ideas presented in previous chapters. The growing importance of team culture is also shared.
- **The Future of Information Architecture**: Chapter 10 identifies IA trends and future directions, including global and increasing AI considerations. We urge practitioners to work together to continue to promote and grow the discipline to help improve people's lives through design. The chapter ends with a revisit of the IA definition used throughout the book.

Washington, DC, USA   Wei Ding
Philadelphia, PA, USA   Xia Lin
Ambler, PA, USA   Michael Zarro

Contents

About the Authors

Dr. Wei Ding is a digital product strategist and program manager with more than 20 years of experience in user experience design, marketing, and consumer behavior. She is currently leading the digital product team at the U.S. Consumer Financial Protection Bureau (CFPB), overseeing the ideation, design, and development of all consumer-facing digital products. Previously she held various design leadership positions at other federal government agencies and private sectors, including the Federal Aviation Administration, U.S. Patent and Trademark Office, Marriott International, and Vanguard. She helped institutions establish user experience design disciplines, and led the successful design/redesign of large-scaled ecommerce or government websites, such as uspto.gov, Marriott.com, and vanguard.com.

Dr. Ding has been an adjunct professor at Drexel University teaching Information Architecture and other graduate level courses since 2006. She has a Ph.D. degree in Information Science from the University of Maryland, and a B.S. and M.S. from Peking (Beijing) University. She has published a number of research papers and articles and is a frequent speaker at professional conferences and industry forums.

Dr. Xia Lin is a Professor in the College of Computing and Informatics at Drexel University. His major research areas include digital libraries, information visualization, information retrieval, and knowledge organization. He initiated the Information Architecture course at Drexel in 2003 and has taught the course for many years.

Dr. Lin has published more than 100 research papers and received significant research grants from federal agencies and industries. His visualization prototypes have been presented and demonstrated in many national and international conferences. Dr. Lin has a Ph.D. in Information Science from the University of Maryland at College Park and a Master of Librarianship from Emory University at Atlanta, Georgia. Prior to join Drexel, Dr. Lin was an assistant professor at the University of Kentucky.

Dr. Michael Zarro is a User Experience executive and strategist with over 20 years of experience in eCommerce, SaaS, and human-centered artificial intelligence applications. Currently he manages a user research and systems thinking practice for Phenom, a global technology company. Dr. Zarro has established several user research teams, designed one of the first product subscription services in eCommerce, and conducted some of the earliest research on social curation.

Dr. Zarro has taught Information Architecture, Information Systems and other graduate courses since 2013. He has published several research articles and presented his work at leading international conferences.

Information Architecture and UX Design: Definitions and Scope

Information architecture (IA) and User Experience Design (UX) is an exciting area of study that is growing in importance in academics, industry, as well as in everyday life. As we all interact with technology—websites, search engines, mobile apps, or smart home devices, why do we have good experience with some of them but not others? Who creates and designs these things that make our life pleasant (or miserable)? How to structure information in a usable way so that we can all find it when we need it? Clearly, it is valuable to study the "space" between human cognitive abilities, information content, and the context of use. Enter Information Architecture and User Experience Design, an interdisciplinary field that is rooted in psychology, ergonomics, user interface design, system design, information organization, information access, and information use.

IA and UX design are critical in many aspects of our world today. While our primary focus will be on web and mobile applications, the principles we discuss are applicable to any digital information space, including medical devices, home automation systems, and more. *We consider the terms IA and UX designer mostly interchangeable* and will use them throughout the book. IA is typically used when working with the information content and structure, while UX designer is used when discussing the user interface and interaction.

In the following chapters, we will explore the growing demand for exceptional design in our society. Our goal is to provide you with the knowledge and skills needed to become capable of creating user-friendly and useful digital experiences.

© The Author(s), under exclusive license to Springer Nature Switzerland AG 2025
W. Ding et al., *Information Architecture and UX Design*, Synthesis Lectures
on Information Concepts, Retrieval, and Services,
https://doi.org/10.1007/978-3-031-72138-0_1

1.1   Definitions of Information Architecture

Information architecture is a field of study, a field of practice, and a discipline that changes as the use of technologies evolves. Like many other evolving disciplines, there exist many definitions of information architecture. Let's start with a look at a few examples of the definitions first.

One cannot talk about information architecture without mentioning Richard Saul Wurman, who coined the term "Information Architecture" or, at least, brought it to wide attention in the 1970s. Wurman was trained as an architect and skilled at graphical design, but "making information understandable" has been "the singular passion of his life." He sees the problems of gathering, organizing, and presenting information as closely analogous to the problems an architect faces in designing a building that will serve the needs of its occupants. His definition of information architects emphasizes the organization and presentation of information (Wurman, 1996):

> (1) the individual who organizes the patterns inherent in data, making the complex clear. (2) a person who creates the structure or map of information which allows others to find their personal paths to knowledge. (3) the emerging 21st century professional occupation addressing the needs of the age focused upon clarity, human understanding, and the science of the organization of information.

While Wurman insightfully bridged information with architecture, Morville et al. (2015) brought information architecture to the mainstream with their popular "polar bear" book on information architecture. In the fourth edition (with Jorge Arango as an additional author), the authors took a multi-perspective approach to define information architecture:

1. The structural design of shared information environments
2. The synthesis of organization, labeling, search, and navigation systems within digital, physical, and cross-channel ecosystems
3. The art and science of shaping information products and experience to support usability and findability, and understanding
4. An emerging discipline and community of practice focused on bringing principles of design and architecture to the digital landscape (p. 24).

This definition provides a focus on structure, cross-channel systems, findability and usability, and finally the spirit of IA—bringing principles of design (art) and architecture (science) to the digital landscape. Resmini and Rosati (2011) similarly emphasize in their definition that, as the *pervasive* information environment evolves, "information architecture was moving into uncharted territories becoming a boundary practice whose contributions were crucial where complexity, unfamiliarity, and information overload stood in the way of the user" (p. 33). IA is a boundary practice that brings together many skills and disciplines. Thus, their definition underscores information architecture as a process and service design, involving designing multi-channel and cross-channel user experience.

1.1.1 Our Definition of IA

In the above, we provide snapshots of different definitions of information architecture. A common theme of IA evolution is from information-centric to user-centric, thus the definition we use in this book:

> Information architecture is about organizing and simplifying information for its intended users; designing, integrating and aggregating information spaces to create usable systems or interfaces; creating ways for people to find, understand, exchange and manage information; and, therefore, stay on top of information and make right decisions.

Information architects not only design individual human-centered *information spaces* (e.g., websites, software, applications, intranets) but through *design thinking* and *systems thinking* (see Chap. 8) also tackle strategic aggregation and integration of multiple information spaces including all channels, modalities, and platforms. They organize information but and simplify it for better understanding using principles from the domains of information organization (Chap. 5), human information behavior (Chap. 6), interaction design (Chap. 7). Finally, the goal of IA is not only to support people finding information but also to manage and use information.

This definition serves as the common theme for all the chapters/topics in this book. At the end of the book, we will revisit this definition again.

1.2 Definitions of User Experience and UX Design

Similar to Information Architecture, there are also many definitions of the ever-evolving User Experience and UX Design. Don Norman is credited with first coining the term user experience in the 1990's while at Apple computer, although the field of design is much older than that (Nielsen, 2017). Prior to the growth of the field due to the rise of personal computers with graphical user interfaces (GUIs) and later the web, UX was practiced (although maybe not with that moniker) in industry settings such as Bell Labs, Xerox Parc, and other organizations. Norman and his colleague Nielsen (1998) offer the following definition: "'User experience' encompasses all aspects of the end-user's interaction with the company, its services, and its products." They also include in the definition:

- Meeting the needs of the customer
- Simplicity and elegance, products that are a joy to own
- UX merges several disciplines, "including engineering, marketing, graphical and industrial design, and interface design." (Nielsen & Norman, 1998).

Hartson and Play in *The UX Book* (2018) define user experience as "the totality of the effects felt by the user before, during, and after interaction with a product or system in an ecology" and further that the job of UX designers "is to design that interaction to create a user experience that is productive, fulfilling, satisfying, and even joyful." (p. 6). Here we see similarities to Nielsen and Norman's definition, that before, during, and after direct interaction matters, and that joy and satisfaction are a component of user experience.

ISO, the International Organization for Standardization, gives us a succinct definition of user experience: "user's perceptions and responses that result from the use and/or anticipated use of a system, product or service." (2019, p. 4). Again, we see that there is more to user experience than just usability or functionality, user's perception is a big part of the outcome, bringing to mind the saying *perception is reality.*

The Interaction Design Foundation (IxDF) helpfully brings together definitions of UX and UX design from an operational standpoint:

> The simplest way to think about user experience design is as a verb and a noun. A UX designer designs (verb)—ideates, plans, changes—the things that affect the user experience (noun)—perceptions and responses to a system or service. (IxDF, 2016)

1.2.1 Our Definition of UX

In all the definitions we see more than just using a system, going beyond the pointing and clicking in an interface to a wider view of meeting user needs and providing a positive perception and satisfaction. Thus, we offer the following definition of user experience:

> User Experience (UX) encompasses all facets of a person's interaction with a system, including their anticipation, engagement, and emotional response. It includes usability, intuition, and user delight, along with the resulting outcomes and perceptions of the system.

1.3   From Web Design to Designing Information Spaces

The rising and rapid evolution of the Web provided many opportunities and challenges for users and designers. These opportunities have expanded even more with mobile, enterprise Software as a Service (SaaS), Generative AI (GenAI) and many more. User needs have expanded from viewing information only to highly interactive actions and contributing to information content and architecture to information spaces. Information architecture gives the *foundation and structure*, while UX design makes the systems *usable and intuitive*.

At the same time, user expectations have risen accordingly. For example, more people expect search engines to be answer engines—giving the answer right away instead of just showing a list of links to webpages. People assume that any answer should be available quickly and the growth of GenAI like ChatGPT, Google's Gemini, Microsoft's Copilot, and Apple's Siri, are a step towards fulfilling this expectation. The online connected space is no longer just made up of hyperlinks for people to browse; it is the place for people to conduct daily activities, connect with others, and experience and influence the world.

As the breadth and depth of people's interaction with the information spaces evolves, the boundaries between the physical world and digital have blurred. The needed IA and design work organizing information, identifying pathways for people to navigate, creating tools and rules for people to arrange information on their own and collaborate with others—becomes so critical and *ubiquitous*. At the same time, because digital systems are so much intertwined with every aspect of people's life, information needs to be relevant and understandable; the space needs to be organized and explorable; the interaction needs to be efficient and engaging; the overall experience needs to be pleasant, effective, engaging, and trustworthy.

To accomplish these goals, IAs and UX designers work closely with many other disciplines to ensure all the issues are taken care of and all challenges are met. Only when all the related disciplines fully leverage their expertise and skill sets, can the overall user experience be realized in the real world (Garrett, 2010).

1.3.1   Related Disciplines

Although many of the related disciplines originated in different contexts aiming to solve different problems, the evolution and expansion of the information society brings them together (Fig. 1.1).

- **Usability Engineering**, which predates the web, is primarily concerned with human–computer interaction, and its goal is to make sure the user interface allows the people to accomplish their tasks effectively, efficiently and satisfactorily.

Fig. 1.1 Disciplines related to IA and UX design

- **Information Science** is a broad interdisciplinary field concerning theories, applications, and technologies related to creation, organization, retrieval, and use of information. Subdomains that are most relevant to IA include user's information needs and information seeking behaviors, information organization and retrieval, and understanding the content and context of information.
- **Human Factors Engineering**, originating from designs of things like airplane pilot's dashboards and physical products, is the discipline of applying what is known about human capabilities and limitations to the design of products, processes, systems, and work environments.
- **Interaction Design** encompasses any design that involves user input and the product's response, including physical and digital devices.
- **Visual Design** clarifies communication and makes information and interaction easier to understand using a visual language, such as colors, shapes, layouts, spacing, alignments and styles.
- Finally, **Information Design** is concerned with how the choice of information provided can influence user behaviors (Bergemann & Morris, 2019).

1.3.2 Information Architects and UX Designers

Job titles, roles, and responsibilities are decidedly not standardized in our domain which you may find ironic, considering this is the group that aims to make things understandable. In practice, terms like UX designer, product designer, and information architect are sometimes used interchangeably. Rosala and Krause (2020) surveyed 963 people in the UX field and found an amazing *134 unique job titles*. Further, they report that 74% of professionals classified as "designers" or "non-specialized" have information architecture responsibilities, illustrating the overlap between roles and titles. At least for the time being, we agree with the sentiment expressed by Teo (2023), "UX roles are in flux—and we predict that they always will be."

In this book we argue that *IA and UX design are two sides of the same user experience coin*. IA is the foundation, the glue that helps keep all the puzzle pieces in a system together while UX design creates an overall positive user experience. Roles or activities do not always correspond to job titles. In a small organization, all activities may be performed by one person (*the UX team of one*), while larger organizations will have specialists. No matter the structure, from a human-centered design process perspective, user experience professionals are involved from the beginning to end:

- They work with the business to help establish business vision and strategy.
- They work to determine research goals and objectives and transform research findings into design concepts.
- They work hand in hand with interaction designers to define the interaction model and system behavior. They determine the system functionality and connections between information objects.
- They work with visual designers to create visioning screens upfront and later convert design concepts into final designs with all visual details (e.g., colors, fonts, images) in place.
- They work with development and testing teams to make sure the design gets implemented and functions as intended.
- They study the interconnected elements and integrate systems to deliver exceptional outcomes.

1.3.3 AI Advancements in IA

Recent advances in Artificial Intelligence (AI) have brought new excitement to the UX field. IA and UX design now works with data scientists and machine learning engineers to create human-centered AI (HCAI) experiences. The formidable capacity of AI expands our understanding of how much more IA can do to enhance people's interaction with contextual information for their daily life, which is a fundamental goal of IA.

Without going into details, here are some advancements that are occurring:

- Advancement in Generative AI has fundamentally changed how contextual information drives the process of question-answering and information seeking (think of ChatGPT, for example).
- Personalized information delivery is reaching a new level based on the AI-powered precision recommendation and dynamic learning of user's information needs (think of the daily enhancement of Netflix or Spotify's personalized recommendation).
- Dynamic LLMs have been adopted to enable automatic classification and categorization of large amounts of information and enhance the label creation process of information organizing (think of ontology and taxonomy creation) (Lin & Chang, 2024).
- Digital self and digital twins development is setting a high bar of coupling of AI and IA. From digital interfaces to digital personas to digital humans, information architecture is required to understand and structure user experience in the digital environment at a completely different level (Campbell & Jovanovic, 2022).

Table 1.1 Many foundational concepts in information architecture and UX design were first published decades ago, and are as relevant today as they were almost a century ago

Concept	Decade
Zipf's law	1940's
Bounded rationality	1950's
Fitt's law	1950's
Hick's law	1950's
Miller's law (7 ± 2)	1950's
Response times	1960's
Berry picking	1980's
Paradox of choice	2000's

1.3.4 Timeless Concepts

Technologies like GenAI move very quickly, while IA and UX are founded on the principles of human-centered design which have not changed substantially in decades (International Organization for Standardization, 2019). Almost without fail, any book on technology has sections that expire after some time, and this work is no exception. However, we focus on the concepts that are *timeless* (Table 1.1) and apply to a broad range of systems, from websites to mobile apps and on to AI. For example, human's perception of system response times has stayed the same for decades, an limitations on decision making like "bounded rationality" (Simon, 1996) has not changed since it was first described in the 1950's, and in fact existed for millennia before that. The core ideas behind research and evaluation methods haven't changed. In short, we think about it like this—*while technology advances rapidly, humans evolve slowly*—thus any work focused on the human user experience will logically focus on lasting principles and practices and remain relevant for years to come. We'll discuss these concepts and more in Chap. 6.

1.4 Summary

Information architecture and UX Design is a field with growing importance across all walks of life, as boundaries between the physical world and digital space blur. The domain can be defined several ways. We define it for this book in terms of designing, organizing, synthesizing, and integrating so that people experience positive outcomes: Being informed, making good decisions, enjoying their interactions, and making progress towards their goals. To accomplish this, designers use time-tested principles and work closely with others, bringing together the pieces of the puzzle needed to create *meaningful, functional, and beautiful information spaces.*

References

Bergemann, D., & Morris, S. (2019). Information design: A unified perspective. *Journal of Economic Literature, 57*(1), 44–95. https://doi.org/10.1257/jel.20181489

Campbell, M., & Jovanovic, M. (2022). Digital self: The next evolution of the digital human. *Computer, 55*(04), 82–86.

Garrett, J. J. (2010). *The elements of user experience: User-centered design for the web and beyond* (2nd ed.). New Riders.

Hartson, R., & Pyla, P. S. (2018). *The UX book: Agile UX design for a quality user experience.* Morgan Kaufmann.

Interaction Design Foundation—IxDF. (2016). What is user experience (UX) design? https://www.interaction-design.org/literature/topics/ux-design.

International Organization for Standardization. (2019). *Ergonomics of human-system interaction—Part 210: Human-centred design for interactive systems* (ISO Standard No. 9241-210:2019). https://www.iso.org/standard/77520.html.

Lin, X. & Chang, X. (2024). *Towards taxonomy management with generative AI.* Presented at the NKOS Workshop, 2024 (March 20–21, the 18th ISKO Conference, Wuhan, China). https://nkos.dublincore.org/2024NKOSworkshops/Lin.TaxonomyManagement.pdf.

Morville, P., Rosenfield, L., & Arango, J. (2015). *Information architecture for the web and beyond* (4th ed.). O'Reilly.

Nielsen, J. (2017). *A 100-year view of user experience.* Nielsen Norman Group. https://www.nngroup.com/articles/100-years-ux/.

Norman, D., & Nielsen, J. (1998). *The definition of user experience (UX).* NNGroup. https://www.nngroup.com/articles/definition-user-experience/.

Resmini, A., & Rosati, L. (2011). *Pervasive information architecture: Designing cross-channel user experiences.* Elsevier.

Rosala, M., & Krause, R. (2020). *User experience careers: What a career in UX looks like today.* NNGroup. https://media.nngroup.com/media/reports/free/UserExperienceCareers_2nd_Edition.pdf.

Simon, H. A. (1996). *The sciences of the artificial.* MIT Press.

Teo, Y. S. (2023). *The ultimate guide to understanding UX roles and which one you should go for.* Interaction Design Foundation—IxDF. https://www.interaction-design.org/literature/article/the-ultimate-guide-to-understanding-ux-roles-and-which-one-you-should-go-for.

Wurman, R. (1996). *Information architects.* Graphis Press.

Information Architecture and Evolving Information Spaces

Online and other digital information spaces are increasingly integrated into everyday life. Today, over 5.4 billion people around the globe (67% of the world's population) are connected to the internet, including a large majority in developed countries and an increasing number in developing countries (International Telecommunication Union, 2023). It seems that more and more time is spent online as formerly offline activities (like depositing a check, booking a flight, paying taxes) move to websites and mobile apps. High speed 5 g cellular networks, WiFi, and mobile devices keep connections alive 24 h a day; while broadband connectivity lets the 1's and 0's that carry information fly around the globe at the speed of light. Mobile, wearables, sensors, artificial intelligence (AI) and *the internet of things* have become a big part of our lives.

Although it only has a relatively short history, the content and look of the World Wide Web (the web, WWW) and internet, as well as information space design and digital technologies in general, have all gone through several generations of changes. In this chapter we will highlight major changes in this evolution; from a domain of the select few to the digitally powered world many of us live in today, with ubiquitous connectivity and where freedom of internet access is considered a basic human right and a "driving force" in development (United Nations General Assembly, 2012).

Activities in information spaces today can be distributed across time and space, where previously they were bound to a time and location, "formerly clear lines are fading away—between online and offline, internal and external, owned and shared, customer and user, social and business" (Guenther, 2013, p. 10). Examples of this include:

W. Ding et al., *Information Architecture and UX Design*, Synthesis Lectures on Information Concepts, Retrieval, and Services, https://doi.org/10.1007/978-3-031-72138-0_2

- Patrons previously went to the library and retrieved physical books for a few weeks. Now, patrons can borrow eBooks online.
- Children used a modem to connect over the family telephone line and signed off so their parents could make a phone call. Now, many homes have dedicated broadband internet access.
- Professionals used to commute to an office every day, now millions of people work "remote" from their homes or other locations.

Information spaces are pervasive and inter-connected (Resmini & Rosati, 2011), accessible anytime and anywhere. Therefore, designers should work to maximize the benefits, while minimizing limitations inherent in each channel or device—a task that can sometimes entail what seems like multiple designs for one project. Ideas like *responsive design* (Marcotte, 2011) and *mobile-first* help maintain a cohesive experience while maintaining learnability, and findability across devices and channels. *Design Thinking* ensures products are human-centered and viable for a business, while *Systems Thinking* takes a 30,000 view and provides the insights needed to make substantial improvements. Although this chapter looks back at past developments, we also see new areas like voice, Generative AI (GenAI), and automated assistants becoming a part of IA in the future.

2.1   From the Web to Generative Information Spaces

The pre-history of the web, including Bush's Memex (1945) and other early ideas around information spaces and information architecture could fill a book of its own. Similarly, many internet developments along the way are left out, like ALOHAnet (Abramson, 1970). According to the W3C World Wide Web Consortium, the first general release of WWW happened on May 17, 1991 (2000). Since then, the web has grown exponentially, with people and devices connecting to each other at an increasing rate while creating, sharing, and consuming information. The web experience was once mostly static content delivered to a user at a computer workstation. Now, interactive content delivered to the user on the device of their choosing is often the norm.

2.1.1   From Foundation to Integration

Early in its history the web was primarily meant for read-only access, where most users consumed information created by relatively few. The overall arc has moved towards more interaction and creation, demonstrated by social media, streaming platforms, Software as a Service (SaaS), and Generative AI (GenAI). These capabilities increased the utility of internet-based technologies and helped create our *information society* which has a "profound impression on the way the world functions" (Executive Secretariat of the World Summit on the Information Society, 2005).

An information society is one where functions of business, education, entertainment, healthcare, government, and other critical areas exist largely in information spaces. We feel this is a fair description of the state of affairs in many parts of the world. The information society developed over the years through many generations of the web, starting with the technological foundation and resulting in today's Generative Information Space.

2.1.2 Generations

The web has undergone several transitions since its release: from a foundational era where many of the *core* internet technologies were invented and available to those in the know, to the more static but publicly available web1.0, the more dynamic web2.0, and highly interactive *integrated* eras. Finally, we land in the *generative* era where humans and machines work in unison to find, create, and deliver information. In Table 2.1 we provide a generalized timeline with selected technology examples that highlight each timeframe. The trend is clear that we are on a trajectory from one of limited access by specialists, to interaction, creation, and connections (almost) everywhere for (almost) everyone.

2.1.3 Foundation

In 1971 a team of engineers drove around Philadelphia night after night in a trailer home stocked with sensitive radio equipment, trying to set up the first working cell phone system. (Gertner, 2012, p. 3)

The foundational generation of the web is when many of the technologies that power the information spaces we take for granted were developed at universities and industrial labs. For the most part these technologies were created by and for researchers and scientists who had a vision of a connected future. The book *Where Wizards Stay Up Late*, by Hafner and Lyon (1998), provides an excellent insight into this time, which can have its spirit of invention characterized by their passage on Ray Tomlinson's inclusion of the @ symbol in email addresses:

"I got there first, so I got to choose any punctuation I wanted," Tomlinson said, "I chose the @ sign." The character also had the advantage of meaning "at" the designated institution. He had no idea he was creating an icon for the wired world.

This was a time of experimentation and discovery, mostly out of sight of the general public. The internet grew out of ARPAnet, a network of connected computers initially

Table 2.1 Evaluation of the information space

	Web 1.0	Web 2.0	Integrated information space	Generative information space
Purpose and motivation	Web presence and e-Commerce	User participation (e.g., wikis, blogs) Harness collective intelligence	Connect data contextually and semantically; Access anytime, anywhere; Connect, create, and share	Large scale analytics and deep learning
Platform	Windows is the platform; Web is supplemental	Web is the "platform"	Content is the "platform" (regardless how it is accessed and where it stored, local, online, or cloud)	LLMs
Major ways of information access	Web directories (e.g. the original Yahoo!) and earlier search engines (e.g. Lycos, InfoSeek, and AltaVista)	Search engine with popularity-based ranking (e.g., Google); Aggregators	Context-sensitive and personalized; Data decoupled from device, linked data over the semantic web	ChatBots & automated assistants
Personalization customization	On individual sites	User controlled customization across sites, e.g., site aggregators	Context sensitive personalization and customization	Contextual based learning
Information architecture	From less structured links to structure provided by the site owner	Emergent IA based on user activities/ participation	Integration of displays, devices, content structure, linked data, and usage data	Semantic structures generated from LLMs
Navigation	In-line links, frames pre-determined navigation	Dynamic navigation based on participation	Context-based browsing and links	AI-guided navigation

(continued)

Table 2.1   (continued)

	Web 1.0	Web 2.0	Integrated information space	Generative information space
Look and feel	Text heavy with some graphics, frames, and tables	Consistent look and feel; branding design; user experience design	Responsive design and interactive interfaces; voice and automated assistants	Verbal and visual interaction
Web and Apps	Page-based application	Server-driven web applications and pre-compiled web applications	Linked web and mobile apps perform many essential functions in society	Language-model-based apps
Content and interaction	From static content to database-backed dynamic content	RIAs without page refreshing	Distributed linked data; second screen, user journeys over time and across devices	Content regeneration Conversational AI
User activities	Building/using multiple sites via directories, portals, or search engines; Information seeking	User contributing content and tags; Communities based on common interests	Interacting with the content connected through multiple sources seamlessly	Interacting with agents; Learning to trust LLMs and identify dis/mis-information; Ethics of generative information

developed for the military and later turned to civilian uses of research and education. Access at this point was mostly limited to people at research centers and universities. Most people had little reason, or ability to connect. Developments like the World Wide Web by Tim Berners-Lee at CERN and opening of the internet to a wider audience (S.272—High-Performance Computing Act of 1991) ushered in the Web1.0 generation.

2.1.4   Web1.0

Web1.0 is characterized by public access to the web—when the internet really became a thing that many people could use. Graphical browsers like Netscape Navigator and Internet Explorer provided access to multimedia content, although limited by low-bandwidth modem connections. Dial-up providers like America Online and Compuserve, web search engines like Lycos, and portals like Yahoo! provided access to websites for school, work, and play over telephone lines that had long served homes and businesses. Email, chat rooms, and instant messenger apps handled interpersonal messages. Millions of people adopted the web as a place for learning, communicating, connecting, and entertainment.

Most web pages were static, consisting of text, links and images (JPG or GIF formats) organized by tables or frames. Little more than hyperlinks connected information resources, users navigated around the web to find what they were looking for. Microsoft Windows remained the main platform for computer use, while the web was supplemental. Very little personalization or customization was possible, although database-backed dynamic content grew in importance.

People did not have access anywhere, anytime. Employees had access at their desks (Fig. 2.1), along with a wired mouse and keyboard, desktop phone, and large CRT monitor. At home, dial-up internet was available. The whole family shared a line and could not use the internet and talk on the phone at the same time. Paper maps were still in vogue and location services were not available, people used to even stop and ask directions from strangers! This was the last era where it was expected that most people were disconnected most of the time.

Many of the technologies and companies we rely on today were first used in this generation, including Google, Wi-Fi, and e-Commerce. Demand for increasingly interactive websites, and the technology to support them, ushered in a fast-changing digital landscape. Improvements in bandwidth, user interfaces, and social media soon paved the way for increased interactivity in the web2.0 generation, where information architecture started to become more and more important.

Fig. 2.1 A photo of the author's desk in the Web1.0 era

2.1.5   Web2.0

"Web2.0" (coined by Tim O'Reilly) marked a turning point in the evolution of the web, setting the stage for integrated information spaces. Although many existed beforehand, web2.0 popularized and made central to the online experience several technologies, including:

- Mashups
- Personalization and aggregators
- Rich Internet Applications
- Tagging and hashtags
- Wikis, blogs, and social media
- SaaS/web office applications.

So many of these technologies are ingrained in our experiences that we do not differentiate by name any longer, they are just part of "the web," a constant part of our information experience. Let's take a brief look at each.

2.1.6   Mashups

Mashups allowed developers to create apps that support users by combining data from separate information spaces into something new (Merrill, 2006; Yu et al., 2008). Web application programming interfaces (APIs) enable sites to share their content for use in mashups, think of it as a way to share only the content, without any user interface design. We show a simple diagram from our original research (Zarro & Lin, 2011) into leveraging social tags to help web searches for health topics in Fig. 2.2. MedlinePlus contains authoritative health content, and a controlled vocabulary of terms. The consumer health site contains data from generally trusted sources—but not to the level of MedinePlus, and user contributed social tags. Creating a mashup with data from both provides a search results page looks like a single standalone app, but behind the scenes the two data sources are combined, or *mashed together*.

APIs consist of *endpoints* that publish data in a format like JSON or XML for other systems to access and reuse (Rodriguez, 2008). Figure 2.3 shows an example of a result for a query sent to the US National Library of Medicine's MedlinePlus endpoint that returned data in XML format. In the query, we asked the API to return results for the term "diabetes" from their Health Topics database. Using HTML, CSS, and other technologies this structured data can be transformed into highly useful information in a user interface.

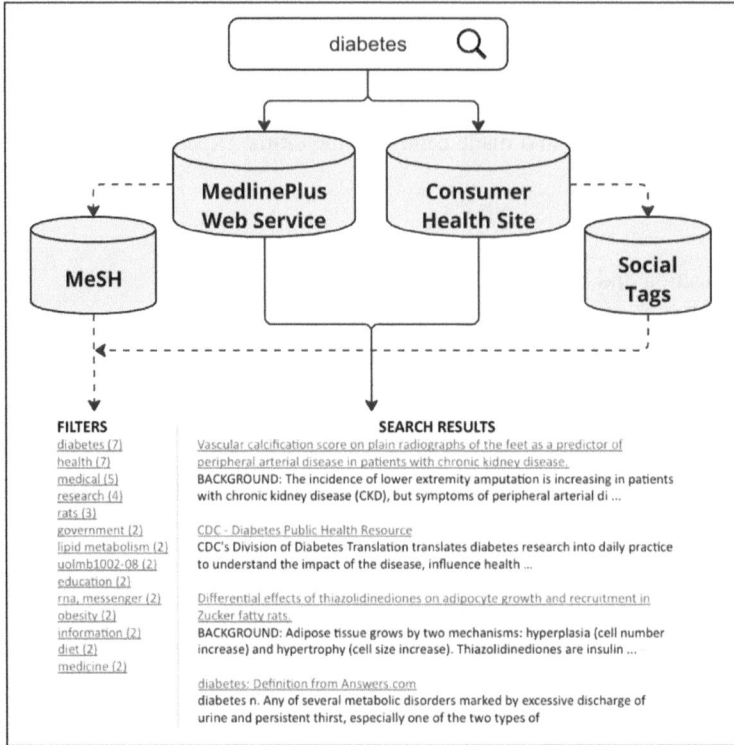

Fig. 2.2 Diagram for a mashup of the US Government's publicly accessible MedlinePlus web service and a consumer health site's API, both providing search results for the query "diabetes." MedlinePlus also contributes medical subject headings (MeSH) while the consumer site contributes social tags. The user sees a single search results page with the combined result set

2.1.7 Personalization and Aggregation

Many sites in the web2.0 generation allowed users to remix and control data that appeared on websites they visited. Users could manually subscribe to news feeds and blogs, add tools or services, and link applications and arrange them in a meaningful way for personal use. On banking websites, for example, users could add their credit cards and billing information, or track investments from different resources. Examples of aggregation websites from this generation include: Netvibes, Pageflakes, iGoogle, and Yahoo! Of these examples, only Yahoo! remains and it is now primarily a news aggregator. In addition to the explicit customization described above, some sites also implemented implicit personalization—tailoring the website content based on a user's profile or activity. A good example of this was Amazon.com's ability to recommend new items based on past purchases at their eCommerce site.

```
– <nlmSearchResult>
    <term>diabetes</term>
    <file>viv_OiMRJo</file>
    <server>pvlbsrch16</server>
    <count>260</count>
    <retstart>0</retstart>
    <retmax>10</retmax>
  – <list num="260" start="0" per="10">
    – <document rank="2" url="https://medlineplus.gov/diabetes.html">
        <content name="title"><span class="qt0">Diabetes</span></content>
        <content name="organizationName">National Library of Medicine</content>
        <content name="altTitle"><span class="qt0">Diabetes Mellitus</span></content>
        <content name="altTitle">Sugar <span class="qt0">Diabetes</span></content>
        <content name="altTitle">DM</content>
      – <content name="FullSummary">
          <p><span class="qt0">Diabetes</span> is a disease in which your blood glucose, or blood sugar, levels are too high.
          Glucose comes from the foods you eat. Insulin is a hormone that helps the glucose get into your cells to give them energy.
          With type 1 <span class="qt0">diabetes</span>, your body does not make insulin. With type 2 <span
          class="qt0">diabetes</span>, the more common type, your body does not make or use insulin well. Without enough insulin,
          the glucose stays in your blood. You can also have prediabetes. This means that your blood sugar is higher than normal but
          not high enough to be called <span class="qt0">diabetes</span>. Having prediabetes puts you at a higher risk of getting type
          2 <span class="qt0">diabetes</span>.</p><p>Over time, having too much glucose in your blood can cause serious
          problems. It can damage your eyes, kidneys, and nerves. <span class="qt0">Diabetes</span> can also cause heart disease,
          stroke and even the need to remove a limb. Pregnant women can also get <span class="qt0">diabetes</span>, called
          gestational <span class="qt0">diabetes</span>.</p><p>Blood tests can show if you have <span
          class="qt0">diabetes</span>. One type of test, the A1C, can also check on how you are managing your <span
          class="qt0">diabetes</span>. Exercise, weight control and sticking to your meal plan can help control your <span
          class="qt0">diabetes</span>. You should also monitor your blood glucose level and take medicine if prescribed.
          </p><p>NIH: National Institute of <span class="qt0">Diabetes</span> and Digestive and Kidney Diseases</p>
        </content>
        <content name="mesh"><span class="qt0">Diabetes Mellitus</span></content>
        <content name="groupName">Seniors</content>
        <content name="groupName">Endocrine System</content>
        <content name="groupName">Metabolic Problems</content>
        <content name="groupName"><span class="qt0">Diabetes Mellitus</span></content>
      – <content name="snippet">
```

Fig. 2.3 Results in XML format for the API query used in the health mashup diagrammed in Fig. 2.3. https://wsearch.nlm.nih.gov/ws/query?db=healthTopics&term=%22diabetes

2.1.8 Rich Internet Apps and Web Office Apps

Rich Internet Apps (RIA) provided methods for users to interact with information over the web (Fraternali et al., 2010). Although the term has fallen out of favor, RIA features are included in many websites and apps today. Imagine trying to use apps without these features:

- Direct manipulation (e.g., drag and drop to move objects/components around on the page).
- Immediate system feedback/messaging for error handling or contextual help.
- Typeahead text predictions.
- Mouseover objects to show additional information.
- Automatic saving of user-entered information.
- Refreshing information on parts of a webpage without having to reload the entire page.

Web office apps provided word processing, spreadsheets and other productivity software through a browser. This connected experience gave users the ability to work on a single document stored online with multiple devices. Office 365 and Google docs are popular examples of web office apps today. Collaboration emerged as a prime benefit, several authors could edit a single document instead of emailing copies back and forth. Rich internet and web office apps helped to pave the way for cloud applications, and the growth of the Software as a Service (SaaS) industry.

2.1.9 Tagging and Hashtags

Tagging gives users the power to label and categorize resources using freely chosen keywords. Compare this to a traditional library, where a professional cataloger assigns a resource into a previously defined category, even when that resource does not fit neatly or addresses several topics. Tags are especially important for categorizing with user-centered, emerging, and event-based keywords, which may not yet (or ever) be in a controlled vocabulary—and in spaces like social media where there is no central cataloging authority. We'll discuss this more in chapter five. Tags have evolved in many systems to "hashtags," (Fig. 2.4) which are labels preceded by the hash or pound symbol "#." However, tags and hashtags may not account for synonyms and other concepts from the library sciences, for example #ux may not always find resources tagged #userexperience. Much like the "@" symbol has been co-opted by email, the hash symbol is now associated with tags.

Fig. 2.4 Hashtags allow for access to related topics (#ia, #library, etc.). Note the repetition of user contributed tags that mean the same thing, like "#ux" and "#userexperience"

2.1.10 Wikis, Blogs, and Social Media

Wikis and blogs are platforms that empower individuals to express themselves, share ideas, receive feedback, and contribute to the public knowledge base in dynamic ways. Wikis, such as Wikipedia, follow a democratic model that allows people to collaboratively work on shared topics of interest. In contrast, blogs enable authors to self-publish articles and other materials, offering a platform for personal expression and creativity. These tools have democratized the web, enabling anyone with an internet connection to contribute their thoughts and ideas. In the corporate world, companies like IBM have researched these tools for internal use by employees (DiMicco et al., 2008).

Social media platforms facilitate connections, communication, and interaction among users. They allow users to share updates, information, images, and videos, while engaging with the activities and content of their networks. These platforms can cater to both general networking and specific interests, with personalization features guiding users to topics and content that interest them. Additionally, *niche social networks*, such as PatientsLikeMe, provide spaces for people with similar medical conditions to share treatment information and emotional support.

2.2   Integrated Generation

Building on the web2.0 era, technologies in the integrated era are generally liberated from a specific device or location. Where at the web's release a computer with a wired connection was required, Wifi and wireless (cellular) networks today provide a connection in most of the developed, and much of the developing world. Mobile continues to grow, a 2024 report by the Pew Research Center finds 90% of people in the US own a smartphone; while South Korea leads the surveyed countries, where a reported 99% of the population own a smartphone (Poushter et al., 2024). In short, many people are almost always within arm's reach of a device with a web connection, ready to search or create new information, connect with friends and colleagues, or be entertained. Sensors and wearables connect and provide information even without explicit interaction, while automobile companies tout their connectivity, technology and over the air software updates. Given the historical trends—expect that all types of connectivity will continue to grow in both developed and developing countries, for all sorts of technologies (Fig. 2.5).

The integrated era was characterized by technologies and concepts, such as:

- Cloud
- Mobile
- Sensors and the internet of things

Fig. 2.5 Integrated
information spaces

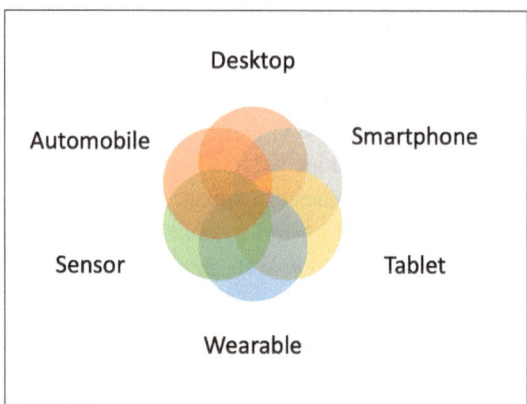

- Wearables
- Ubiquity and User-Centered
- Artificial intelligence/automated assistants.

2.2.1   Cloud

Cloud computing provides two major benefits. First, access to large amounts of storage and second, access to powerful computer processing hardware over the internet. Web office apps, games, and others took advantage of these capabilities. The entire SaaS industry, for example, is built to provide business services "in the cloud" to millions or billions of users. As software and storage is no longer limited to a user's device, new opportunities for collaboration open. Additionally, startups can leverage enterprise class hardware without great up-front costs, opening the door for entrepreneurs to launch innovative businesses at a large scale. Cloud also means updates can be pushed to clients without them need to install anything new. Major cloud providers include: Amazon AWS, Microsoft Axure, and Google Cloud.

2.2.2   Mobile

Mobile devices are almost everywhere today making it hard to believe that they are a relatively new invention. Beginning with the release of the iPhone in 2007 (although devices like Blackberry preceded it), smartphones became mainstream devices. Supported by cellular data, mobile devices took off quickly and now account for a large percentage of user's screen time. In fact, many people reach for a smartphone even when a more capable device like a laptop computer is nearby. Mobile opened up a whole new world of interactions for IAs to explore, including components like GPS and cameras, apps able to leverage those components in new ways, and as an always on device they support push notifications and event-based interactions. Advances in mobile networking like 5G has only made this more powerful and pervasive. Because mobile devices are not typically shared, they readily support personalization and customization.

2.2.3   Sensors and the Internet of Things (IoT)

Perhaps the best experience with information spaces is one in which the technology seems to "disappear" (Weiser, 1991). In addition to systems supporting information creation and consumption by human users, sensors and the internet of things opens a new world of *invisible information architecture* by connecting items like automobiles, home thermostats, and even refrigerators to the web. Advances in medical devices and similar products can have a profound impact on the quality of life for patients, while blockchain technologies combined IoT are driving advances in the transportation industry and supply chain management.

2.2.4   Wearables

Wearables, like Fitbits and Apple watches, generally needed to connect with another device like an iPhone to perform all their functions. Sometimes they are used to collect biometric data, like heart rate, and watches are where text messages and alerts appear for many people. Wearables are now part of the information landscape and will likely become more popular. They should be considered in projects as an opportunity to expand IA, taking into account their unique interface.

2.2.5   Ubiquity and Human-Centered

In developed countries there is an expectation that most people are connected—access to the internet is nearly *ubiquitous*. Tax forms and other government documents are online. Banking and essential services are conducted through online apps. Tickets to sporting events and concerts are delivered to digital wallets. On a college campus, students search for resources on a library website and download them instantly. For most technologies it is probably more common for a device to be connected than not, providing opportunities for IAs to leverage the capabilities brought about by broadband, cloud, and other technologies.

   Ubiquity heightens the need for IAs and UX designers to get involved in many aspects of society, work, and daily life. Human-centered design (Chap. 3) supports many users' ability to leverage these futuristic technologies, a far cry from web1.0 where the web was "read only" for most people. This leads us to the following Generative generation, where we see an even deeper collaboration between human and computer enabled by more and more advanced AI capabilities.

2.2.6 Artificial Intelligence, Automated Assistants

In a world of information overload, technology helps us sift through the noise to find what we want. The ever-growing landscape of technologies led to the development of increasingly *smarter* assistants or agents (Maes, 1994). Popular AI-powered assistants included Siri (Apple), Alexa (Amazon), Cortana (Microsoft), and Watson (IBM). These assistants were designed to appear intelligent, utilizing machine learning and artificial intelligence to efficiently complete routine tasks and provide answers that users may not easily find on their own. In fields like medicine, IBM's Watson aided doctors by analyzing symptoms and suggesting possible diagnoses, while in the home, assistants automated tasks, reminders, and other aspects of daily life. Although these are quite powerful in their own right; later advances in GenAI like ChapGPT greatly expanded the capabilities of AI tools, leading all AI-focused companies to keep up (e.g., Google Gemini and Microsoft Co-Pilot) in the following Generative generation.

2.3 Generative Generation

This generation of information spaces is marked by the rapid development of generative AI. The increasing complexity of the spaces brings both excitement and challenges to the field of information architecture. IA professionals are working to make generative AI a mighty member of the IA team and *leverage AI tools to enhance their IA and UI/UX workflows*. For example, with the huge amount of information readily available through large language models (LLMs), ChatGPT is an excellent assistant in streamlining the IA processes and offering suggestions or recommendations for creating effective UI/UX architecture designs. ChatGPT has been used to help the UX designer to do market research, develop wireframes, and analyze user's feedback. Once time-consuming IA work now can be done much more effectively.

Generative information spaces contain data and information generated, produced, or reproduced by both humans and the increasingly powerful artificial intelligence artifacts. Due to the inherent issue of inaccuracy in the pre-trained LLMS, data and information generated by the models might include facts or fiction. GenAI has been said to *hallucinate*, providing incorrect or non-sensical results. Never before have we faced the amount of information rushing back and forth that might be inaccurate, fake, or misleading. A new challenge for IAs and UX designers is how to work with the LLM models, both guiding and being guided by them, to create information structures or user interfaces to help users in identifying, limiting, and managing misinformation or disinformation. Meaningful means need to be developed to assist the users in understanding whether certain information is trustworthy. An example of such means is the integration of GenAI and knowledge graphs. Another is the development of new methods for systematically assessing risks of AI artifacts.

Another major development that has a significant impact to information architecture is the human-centered explainable AI (XAI) (Xu et al., 2019). Humans need to co-exist with AI in the generative information spaces. Nevertheless, with a "black box" (Dobson, 2023) of deep learning, LLM-based AI artifacts are incapable of explaining their actions, their reasoning or the sources of information. Rather than attempting to open the black box, human-centered XAI aims to explore a holistic vision of AI explainability and study factors outside of the black box to boost the explainability of AI. It works on the human and sociotechnical sides in seeking understanding of AI's behaviors. Back to the field of information architecture, the human-centered XAI is applied to determine the role of generative AI in the IA process, through the RACI model – Responsible, Accountable, Consulted, and Informed. What is the generative AI responsible for and accountable for in the process of IA/UX design? This is the question that will continue to be defined, explored, and learned.

2.4 Summary

This chapter presents the digital landscape through the generations of Web and information spaces. Table 2.2 highlights the evolution.

Information technology is an industry of constant change and disruption. It is important to look back and understand that human beings invented all the technologies we take for granted, and today we build on what has come before. Information Architects will have a large hand in *inventing the future* and should learn to adapt and leverage the right technologies in the right contexts, while also keeping an eye towards creating the new and unexpected. ChatGPT, Human-centered Explainable AI, and disinformation management

Table 2.2 Evolution of information spaces

Generations	Main challenges
The web 1.0 generation	Information scarcity
The web 2.0 generation	Information overload
The integration generation	Semantic linking
The generative generation	Accountability and truthfulness

are three landmarks in the generative generation of information spaces that will have significant impact to the field of IA and UX design. The rapid development of generative AI will continue to reshape the evolving information spaces, fostering more innovative and creative approaches within the IA domain.

References

Abramson, N. (1970). The Aloha system: Another alternative for computer communications. In: *Proceedings of the November 17–19, 1970, Fall Joint Computer Conference* (pp. 281–285). ACM. https://doi.org/10.1145/1478462.1478502.

Bush, V. (1945). *As we may think*. The Atlantic. Retrieved from http://www.theatlantic.com.ezp roxy2.library.drexel.edu/magazine/archive/1945/07/as-we-may-think/3881/?single_page=true.

DiMicco, J. M., Millen, D. R., Geyer, W., Dugan, C., & Street, O. R. (2008). Research on the use of social software in the workplace. In *Conference Proceedings* (pp. 8–12). Citeseer.

Dobson, J. E. (2023). On reading and interpreting black box deep neural networks. *International Journal of Digital Humanities, 5*(2), 431–449.

Executive Secretariat of the World Summit on the Information Society. (2005). *World summit on the information society*. Retrieved December 10, 2016, from https://www.itu.int/net/wsis/basic/faqs.asp.

Fraternali, P., Rossi, G., & Sánchez-Figueroa, F. (2010). Rich internet applications. *IEEE Internet Computing, 14*(3), 9–12. https://doi.org/10.1109/MIC.2010.76

Gertner, J. (2012). *The idea factory*. Penguin.

Guenther, M. (2013). *Intersection: How enterprise design bridges the gap between business, technology, and people*. Morgan Kaufmann.

Hafner, K., & Lyon, M. (1998). *Where wizards stay up late: The origins of the Internet*. Simon and Schuster.

International Telecommunication Union (ITU). (2023). *Facts and figures 2023—Internet use*. https://www.itu.int/itu-d/reports/statistics/2023/10/10/ff23-internet-use.

Maes, P. (1994). Agents that reduce work and information overload. *Communications of the ACM, 37*(7), 30–40.

Marcotte, E. (2011). *Responsive web design*. A book apart.

Merrill, D. (2006). Mashups: The new breed of web app. *IBM web architecture technical library* (pp. 1–13).

Poushter, J., Gubbala, S., & Austin, S. (2024). 8 charts on technology use around the world. *Pew research*. https://www.pewresearch.org/short-reads/2024/02/05/8-charts-on-technology-use-around-the-world/.

Resmini, A., & Rosati, L. (2011). *Pervasive information architecture: Designing cross-channel user experiences*. Elsevier.

Rodriguez, A. (2008). Restful web services: The basics. *IBM developer works*.

S.272—High-Performance Computing Act of 1991. (1991). S.272—High-performance computing act of 1991. https://www.congress.gov/bill/102nd-congress/senate-bill/272.

United Nations General Assembly. (2012). *Human rights council twentieth session—A/HRC/20/L.13*. United Nations. https://documents-dds-ny.un.org/doc/UNDOC/LTD/G12/147/10/PDF/G12 14710.pdf?OpenElement.

W3C. (2000). *A little history of the world wide web*. https://www.w3.org/History.html.

Weiser, M. (1991). The computer for the 21st century. *Scientific American, 265*(3), 94–104.

Xu, F., Uszkoreit, H., Du, Y., Fan, W., Zhao, D., & Zhu, J. (2019). Explainable AI: A brief survey on history, research areas, approaches and challenges. In: J. Tang, M. Y. Kan, D. Zhao, S. Li, & H. Zan (Eds.), *Natural language processing and Chinese computing*. NLPCC 2019. Lecture Notes in Computer Science, vol. 11839. Springer, Cham. https://doi.org/10.1007/978-3-030-32236-6_51.

Yu, J., Benatallah, B., Casati, F., & Daniel, F. (2008). Understanding mashup development. *IEEE Internet Computing, 12*(5), 44–52.

Zarro, M. & Lin, X. (2011). Using social tags and controlled vocabularies as filters for searching and browsing: A health science experiment. *The fifth workshop on human-computer interaction and information retrieval (HCIR2011), mountain view.*

Human-Centered Design

3

Information architects (IAs) and UX designers help to create a *human-centered* future, where the user's goals and needs serve as the guidelines for design and development. Human-centered design (HCD) is a framework that places people as the center of focus during the whole design process. In this approach, designers and other stakeholders identify people's needs and balance them with business and technical concerns, to improve usability and maximize the outcomes of an information space (Fig. 3.1).

Human-centered design expands on the previously popular term *user-centered* design. In chapters three through eight we cover concepts relating to HCD. For those new to IA and UX design (like the students we taught for many years) descriptions of our field may sometimes sound like a word salad, consisting of "human," "user," "people," "design," "experience," "centered," and finally "thinking." The key takeaway is to always keep HCD top of mind, focus on the impact your design has on the person using it and others, and use the appropriate methods throughout the design process.

3.1   Human-Centered Design Background

Human-centered design aims to make systems usable and useful by focusing on people and their needs by applying human factors/ergonomics, and usability knowledge and techniques. Digital systems have expanded well beyond websites and apps (the main focus of our book), making HCD an important concept for many industries where user experience impacts user and business outcomes (Norman, 2002). HCD enhances usability, improves human well-being, accessibility and sustainability; and counteracts possible

© The Author(s), under exclusive license to Springer Nature Switzerland AG 2025   29
W. Ding et al., *Information Architecture and UX Design*, Synthesis Lectures
on Information Concepts, Retrieval, and Services,
https://doi.org/10.1007/978-3-031-72138-0_3

Fig. 3.1 Human-centered
design components: IAs should
look to balance what people
want or need, with the
business' ability to provide it
and the technical ability to
create it

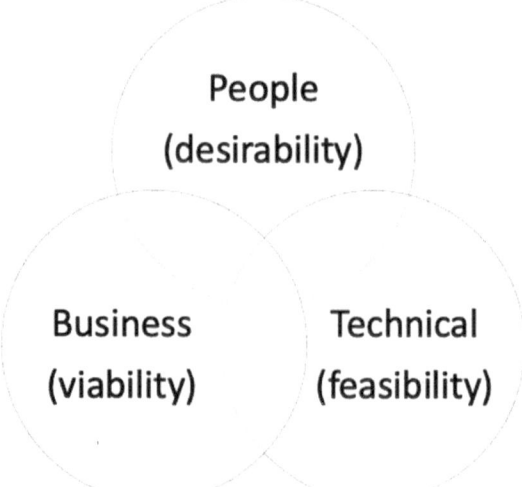

adverse effects of use on human health, safety and performance. The International Organization for Standardization (ISO) (2019) defines HCD as an "approach to systems design
and development that aims to make interactive systems more usable by focusing on the
use of the system and applying human factors/ergonomics and usability knowledge and
techniques" (p. 2).

ISO also shares how human-centered design and user-centered design are often used
synonymously—and we take the same approach in our work. The terminology is less
important than the intent. The thing that matters is to include people in the design while
putting their needs and goals at the center of the work.

While ISO talks of applying methods, the design firm IDEO zooms out to a more
general view, defining human-centered design as "a process that starts with the people
you're designing for and ends with new solutions that are tailor-made to suit their needs"
(IDEO, n.d.).

With all this focus on users and people, do we really understand who they are? They
can be customers or employees, current users or potential users, public users or internal
users, experts or novices, early adopters or technophobes; we think you get the point.
People are multifaceted and change over time. A novice can become an expert, or a person
is happy one moment and angry the next. Part of the design process is identifying and
prioritizing "personas" (Cooper, 2004; Pruitt & Grudin, 2003), to humanize this concept
of system users, and coming up with creative solutions that serve their needs. For the
purposes of this work, we offer the following definition of a user.

User defined: A person interacting with information space(s) to achieve a goal, in the context of work, information seeking or creating, entertainment, or play. They may be experts or novices, experienced or inexperienced, motivated or disinterested. Like all humans, they will have a range of cognitive, psychological, and physical abilities and limitations, and will have moods and preferences that vary over time.

3.2 Include Users in Research and Design

While in the past the user was too-often ignored, today gathering user input early and often is considered best practice. HCD emphasizes research, design, and evaluation as three iterative activities that should be embedded in every stage of design and development (Fig. 3.2). Design and development frameworks, like design sprints (Google Ventures, 2019), or design thinking (Meinel & Leifer, 2023), which we discuss in Chap. 8, are grounded in HCD concepts.

The human user is easily overlooked when designing information systems. Many stakeholders (such as business sponsors or engineers) think, "we know our users, we know what they want" or they listen to the loudest, but not most representative users ("the squeaky

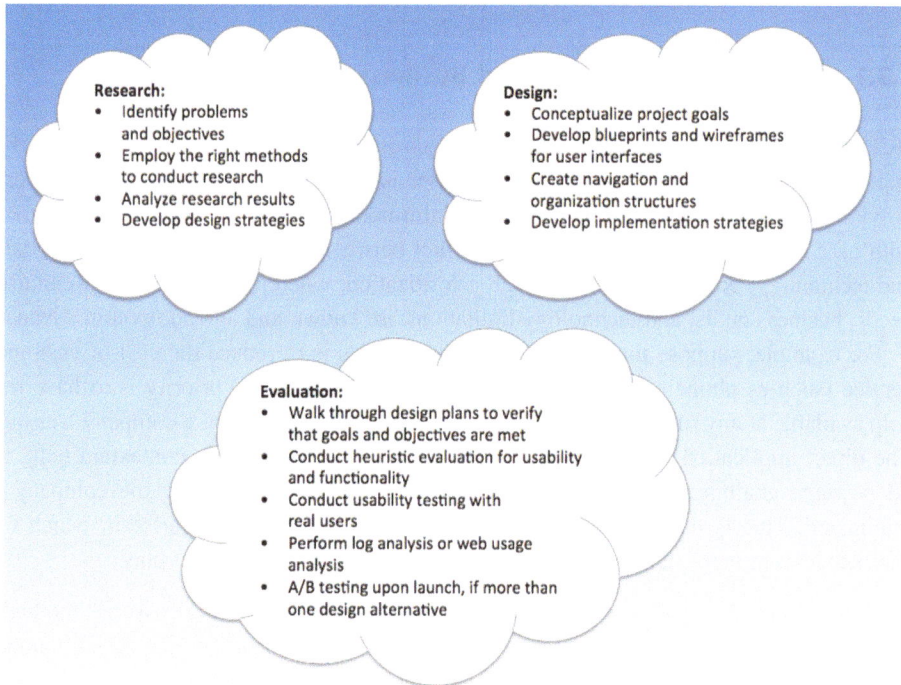

Fig. 3.2 Three clouds of the HCD research

wheel gets the grease" syndrome). This leads to unnecessary rework fixing problems that should have been identified in the early design phase of a project, substandard systems released for use, the need for expensive follow-up customer support, and unhappy users. HCD goes a long way towards avoiding these issues and has been adopted by organizations that see it as the way to build systems with increased adoption by consumers and return on investment (Ross, 2014; Whitten & Bentley, 2007).

HCD puts the user in the center. However, it does not minimize the influence of other stakeholders. Designers and user researchers, due to their unique position creating the system, often serve as the "voice of the user" in an organization while leading HCD processes. We will discuss ISO 9241 and usability from a user standpoint along with a general HCD process in this chapter. In later chapters we will dive into research, design and evaluation. Before we do that, we need some discussions to clarify misconceptions about HCD, and concepts to increase its reach.

3.3   Increasing the Reach of HCD

HCD has many benefits for both users/customer and the business. We share some below, and dispel misconceptions that may hinder organizations from adopting an HCD approach.

3.3.1   Combines User Needs and Business Goals

HCD does not mean focusing only on user needs and ignoring business goals and market opportunities. Rather, HCD means that the user is given a voice in the design process, providing information needed to make well-informed decisions and align business goals with user needs. How do you resolve a conflict between the user needs, business goals, and technology? Reconcile them through prioritization, where the tradeoffs between user needs, business goals, and technology limitations are known and agreed upon in advance.

For example, suppose that one of the business goals is to reduce the cost of customer service (such as phone calls to a call center), whereas the users' priority is to have live help available at any time. What are the implications for the design of a company website? The direct implication is to provide easy-to-use, easy-to-understand, contextual help, an AI powered chatbot, and knowledge base so that the need for calling the company is minimized. This is the ideal situation, but some scenarios may still arise in which the user needs even more help. Here is where the prioritization comes into play.

Option 1 is based on the conclusion that the business goal of reducing costs has the highest priority. Therefore, we may decide not to make any customer service phone number or live chat features easily accessible. For example many e-Commerce sites provide step-by-step instructions for common help needs, reducing the need for customer service calls or chat (Fig. 3.3).

Fig. 3.3 Help section on an e-Commerce site with help categories and no easy "contact us" option—but links to answer common questions

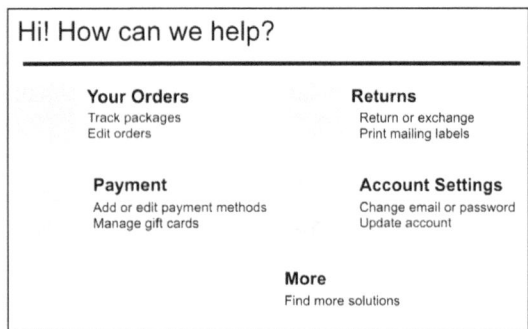

Option 2 is based on the opposite conclusion, that the user's desire for live help is the priority, and always having contact information easily accessible is the right design. However, this will increase the need for more customer care representatives to handle the extra calls and chats, increasing the business costs.

Which one is the right choice? It really depends on the situation. Depending on the business model and culture, some companies (e.g., financial companies) are more likely to think direct contact increases opportunities to earn more business from users; so here making it easy to call the company wins. Other companies may deem cutting costs for customer support as the first business priority, so keeping phone numbers and chat off the site wins. There is not a right or wrong answer that will satisfy everyone in every situation. Part of the designer's role is to balance competing factors and help the team prioritize.

3.3.2 HCD Helps New Technology Adoption

HCD does not mean that the design is against introducing new technologies or changes. New technologies must be incorporated intelligently, while serving a purpose, not just for their own sake. At the same time, it is critical for design professionals to learn the capabilities of newly available technologies and leverage them to improve the user experience and design.

Advances in artificial intelligence (AI) drastically change system capabilities and how people interact with a system. Managing changes like this is always a challenge. For example, how does an IA design a system where the AI synthesizes thousands of sources to give a single answer versus the typical search engine results page with ten blue links? How does a designer provide for "human-in-the-loop" so that humans guide AI responses, making them better over time? How do we design explainable AI (XAI) so people can trust the results? The key is to find the best match between problems at hand and the right technology, balancing features and learnability, with the need to drive technology forward.

3.3.3 Guides Design Ideas

HCD does not mean that users themselves can best design for their own use. Users are usually very good at telling what problems they have, but they do not necessarily always have good solutions. A famous quote has been attributed to Henry Ford: "If I would have asked my customers what they wanted, they would have asked for a faster horse." This means that while users may be able to identify problems they face, they do not always have the expertise, experience, or creativity to come up with innovative solutions that may solve those problems. The designer's responsibility is to understand user problems and needs and transform them into robust design solutions.

3.3.4 Human-Centered AI

The growth of AI applications in a variety of domains has been typically driven by a technology-centered approach, where humans are the second thought. However, the increasing intersection of AI and society gives IAs and designers the opportunity and obligation to guide the development of human-centered AI (HCAI) tools and products. HCAI takes into account the implications, both positive and negative, of AI on society and individual humans (Capel & Brereton, 2021). Today universities like Stanford (https://hai.stanford.edu/) and UC Berkeley (https://humancompatible.ai/) have established HCAI research programs to investigate this new human-centered domain. Governments around the world are likewise keeping an eye on the growing impact of AI.

Human-centered AI systems are designed to work with, and for, people (Barmer et al., 2021). HCAI for designers means applying the human-centered process to AI applications. Shneiderman (2020a), an influential HCI researcher who's written extensively on the topic, claims "HCAI systems emerge when designers, software engineers, and managers adopt user-centered participatory design methods by engaging with diverse stakeholders." (p. 2). Further, Shneiderman (2020b) offers additional ideas for reframing AI into a more human-centered focus:

- "High levels of human control AND high levels of automation are possible" (p. 115): Meaning to determine on a continuum where control should be weighted towards the human (such as a camera where the user points the camera and the software helps eliminate shaking), and where automation should be in control (such as deploying an airbag in a crash).

- "Shift from emulating humans to empowering people" (p. 116): Moving us away from making AI look or sound like humans as a goal (e.g., humanoid robots) that may not be the most effective design and focusing on outcomes of the AI with a goal-centered design.
- "Governance structures for HCAI" (p. 118): In order to join ethical concerns and practice, follow these three practices; use reliable software development methods, develop a culture of safety in the organization, and establish independent oversight.

Similar concepts are found in Xu's (2019) framework for HCAI that has the goal of guiding "safe, efficient, healthy, and satisfying HAI solutions" (p. 44), with additional emphasis on the role of design.

- "Ethically aligned design" (p. 44), for solutions that are fair, just, and do not replace humans.
- "Technology enhancement" (p. 44), to reflect more human-like intelligence.
- "Human factors design" (p. 44), ensuring that AI outcomes are usable and understandable.

We are at the dawn of a new era where AI applications will have an ever increasing influence on design, society, and business. As we will see throughout the remaining chapters, IAs and UX designers are well suited to provide the crucial HCD perspective needed to make AI work for humans.

3.4   ISO 9241

How does an IA put HCD principles into practice? Fortunately, the concepts behind HCD are codified in the ISO-9241-210:2019 standard: *Ergonomics of human-system interaction Part 210: Human-centred design for interactive systems.* ISO describes the concepts, hardware design, software design, and the design processes related to HCD, while also defining several important terms for IA, including a useful and concise definition of usability.

Usability is the core concept when designing for users. ISO 9241 defines usability as the "extent to which a system, product or service can be used by specified users to achieve specified goals with effectiveness, efficiency and satisfaction in a specified context of use" (p. 3). In order to make usability actionable, let's examine the three components and ISO's definitions of each (Table 3.1).

Table 3.1 ISO definitions and examples

ISO definition	Example user metrics
Effectiveness: "Accuracy and completeness with which users achieve specified goals" (p. 2)	Task completion rates, e.g., "7 of 10 (70%) users successfully logged into the system, 3 of 10 (30%) failed"
Efficiency: "Resources used in relation to the results achieved" (p. 2)	Time on task/number of clicks needed to complete task, e.g., "users took on average 7 s to complete login"
Satisfaction: "Extent to which the user's physical, cognitive and emotional responses that result from the use of a system, product or service meet the user's needs and expectations" (p. 3)	User-reported ratings of a system, e.g., "the system scores a 77 out of 100 on our usability scale"

By measuring effectiveness, efficiency, and satisfaction IAs can track performance and improvements (or the opposite!) in ways that are understandable to others in the design field and business stakeholders. It's not just about "make it easy to use" or "make it usable,"—we can quantify usability metrics and objectively show how our systems perform.

Here's an example from industry, to show how usability can have a real-world impact. Imagine a large software enterprise with tens of thousands of employees who often must find information on a company intranet. Employees complain that finding information is difficult and takes a lot of time, and managers notice that even the top performing teams are sometimes not prepared. An exploratory investigation shows that employees often take several hours to find information critical to their jobs. Clearly, the information is not easily accessible. However, the company faces stiff competition and needs to improve the products that it sells. Making the intranet more usable seems to be a poor allocation of the company's IA efforts, which could be used to create better selling software products. The employees just need to get better at finding things, right?

In fact, when we consider ISO's definitions, balancing the usability of the intranet against other priorities becomes easier. Estimating that an improved intranet can save one hour per week per employee by helping them find what they need faster (increasing efficiency), we can judge the benefits the company will see versus the cost to redesign. Measuring the average time it takes to find documents before a redesign, and comparing it to the time it takes afterwards shows the impact of the UX work—when employees are more efficient the company saves money. To go further, we could look at the effectiveness of the intranet. What happens if a salesperson cannot find important documents that will help them close the sale, or a software developer cannot find documentation that explains how a system works and writes code that has a lot of bugs? What would the loss to the company be then? And all of this has not even touched on satisfaction yet. Happy employees are generally productive employees.

Taken together, a redesign of the intranet may be a great business decision due to improved productivity. By applying the concepts of effectiveness, efficiency, and satisfaction the benefits become clear. In fact, some organizations even go so far as to mandate internal systems must be redesigned if they score below a certain threshold on a widely accepted usability scale, to help maintain a high level of employee happiness and productivity.

3.5   HCD Design Process

HCD includes design of things the user sees (front end, user interface) and design of things the user will never see (back end, behind the scenes). Think about it like a car, the engine is almost never seen but has a huge impact on performance, while the steering wheel is always seen and has the biggest impact on user control of the direction. Figure 3.4 illustrates a HCD design process for information architecture. There are two parallel processes in design:

- The front-end user interface (UI) design
- The behind-the-scenes metadata and controlled vocabulary design.

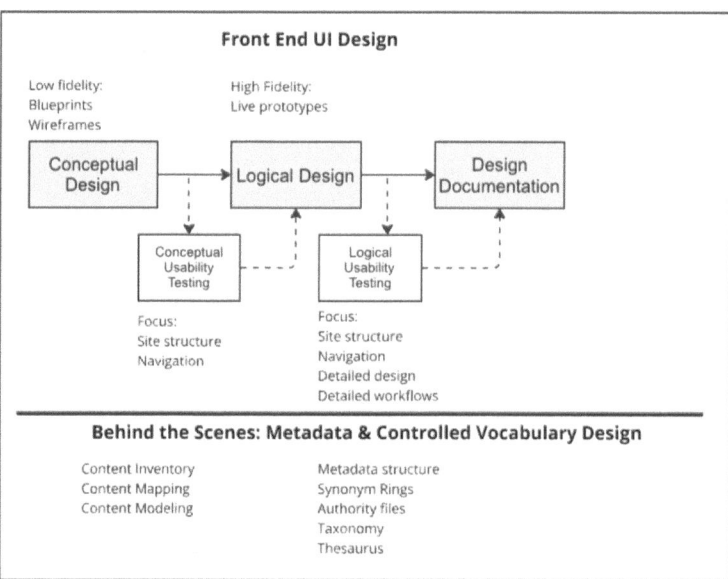

Fig. 3.4 Detailed view of the design process with two parallel processes, front end and behind the scenes

In most cases, the two should go hand in hand. For example, when designing a search capability, the UI piece looks fairly simple (search box, results display), but the majority of the work is behind the scenes in metadata and content. Without appropriate metadata schema, search engine indexing, keywords, relevance ranking mechanism, or controlled vocabulary, search would fail. This parallel work is very visible in a faceted search interface (Hearst, 2009; Tunkelang, 2009), where metadata is placed directly in the UI as filters which the user can apply to limit their search results to specific terms.

3.5.1   Front End UI Design

The upfront UI design involves IAs and UX designers along with visual designers, user researchers, and others. While the UI design evolves and iterates, it is meaningful to differentiate the high-level conceptual design from the more detailed logical design. The beginning conceptual design is more focused on the site structure and navigation—whether the user can easily tell where they are or what they can do, whether the labels make sense, and where else they can go from here. Visual details and specific interactions are handled during logical design—which is closer to the final look of the interface users will see.

Usability tests are recommended at the end of each sub-phase to examine the design with a sample of targeted users. The feedback is then incorporated into the iteration. Testing an interface early means that problems can be identified and fixed more easily and less expensively than finding them later—it's faster, cheaper, and easier to change a wireframe than a fully coded live prototype. Finding the correct users to test with is very important; they must match the characteristics of the projected users for the final product.

3.5.2   Behind the Scenes: Metadata and Controlled Vocabulary Design

Information architects and content people do most of the work behind the scenes developing content and its related metadata and taxonomy. This work is often performed in parallel with UI design. Here, we see the dual-roles IAs and UX designers can play—designing the front end and working behind the scenes as well. On small or medium projects one person may do both, while on larger projects it will take a team.

Metadata and taxonomy development (see Chap. 5) directly informs the design of the navigation and has a big impact on the user experience. Methods like content inventories, card sorting, and tree testing (see Chap. 4) can all be used to create and evaluate the behind the scenes IA work, with the goal of matching user's mental models of an information space with the structure created by IAs. This can be quite challenging and has long been studied in the library sciences.

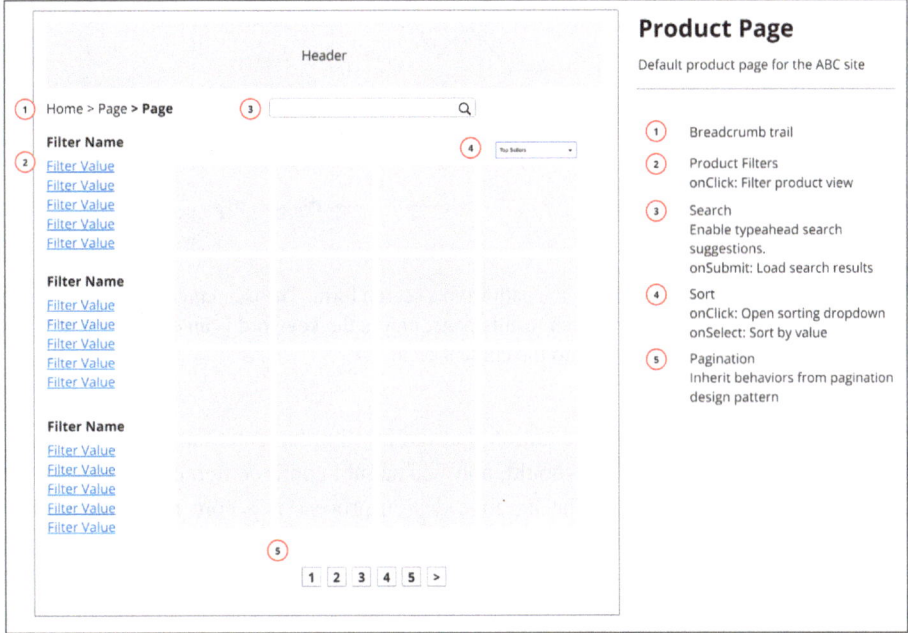

Fig. 3.5 Example low-fidelity wireframe showing a simple product page. On the right are annotations that describe the functionality called out in the screen (#1, 2, 3, etc.)

3.5.3 Design Deliverables

IAs and UX designers, along with other experts, create many deliverables during the design phase, used by the team to develop and communicate designs:

- **For conceptual design**: Wireframe (low-fidelity screens, Fig. 3.5), user-flow diagrams (Fig. 3.6), blueprints (or high-level IA diagram, Fig. 3.7), storyboards.
- **For logical design**: Detailed and interactive prototypes. Used for various design reviews and user tests.
- **Final documentation**: UI specification document, detailed navigation diagram, and detailed IA diagram. They are meant for the developers to fully implement the design.

3.6 Iterative Design

"I have not failed. I've just found 10,000 ways that won't work."—Thomas Edison

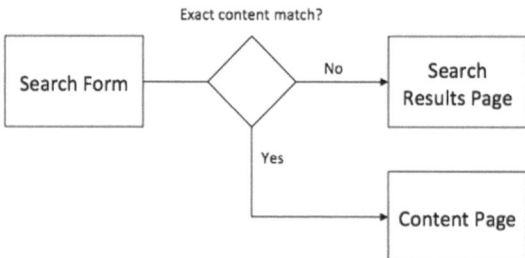

Fig. 3.6 Example user flow showing the path from a search form. The user enters a search term, and the system logic takes them to a search results page, unless the keyword is an exact content match, in which case the system takes them to the content page

Iterative design is based on the notion that the first implementation of a user interface will likely not work as well as it should, and you should continue iterating until it is right (Buxton & Sniderman, 1980). The iterative design process is a core principle of HCD. While we typically show the design process in a linear fashion, in reality the IA may revisit conceptual design and logical design several times, while working towards the optimum design. Buxton and Sniderman (1980) and Nielsen (1993) described iterative computer interface design as a process of prototyping, testing, evaluating results, and refining. Incremental improvements of a single, improving, interface towards a state of completion is the goal. Iterative design has been widely embraced by the UX and startup communities. The fundamentals remain since first described: *You are unlikely to get it right the first time, test with users to see what's not working, fix what doesn't work, and test again until it is right.*

3.7   HCD Teams

Creating complex information spaces requires an interdisciplinary team involving business sponsors, user researchers, visual designers, software developers, project managers, content writers and others. With so many "stakeholders," in order for everyone to collaborate effectively, roles and responsibilities should be made clear. The process may vary from project to project, but the goal should be the same: *Increase the business value of the design and meet the user needs.*

In many organizations, HCD is embedded into the overall product development process. While IAs and designers create UX deliverables, product owners and others gather business and technical requirements. Conceptual designs are often used to guide the requirement gathering activities, and the requirements in turn help refine the design. In our experience as IAs in technology organizations, the IA and product team work closely together cross-referencing requirements and conceptual designs—even going so far as using a checklist to make sure all requirements are met in design.

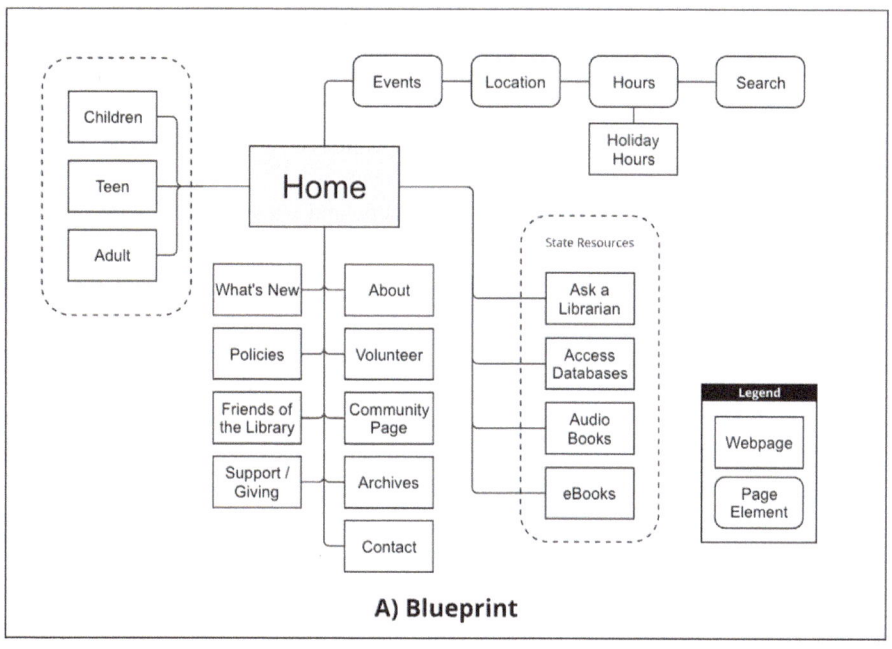

A) Blueprint

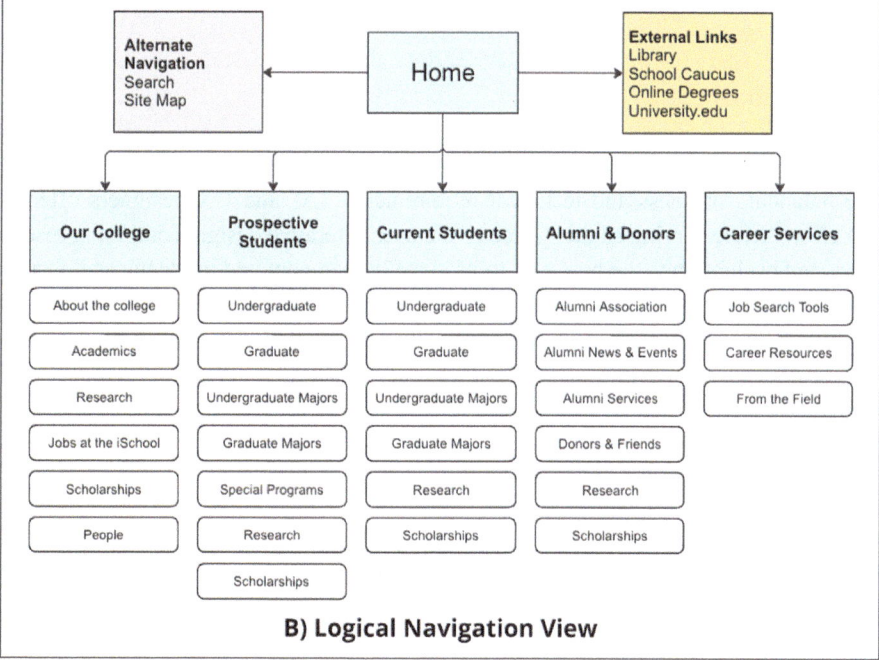

B) Logical Navigation View

Fig. 3.7 Examples of IA deliverables, **a** Blueprint and **b** Logical navigation

Only after business requirements are officially gathered, reviewed and finalized, can the IT team make realistic commitments to the level of effort needed. Requirements and acceptance criteria will greatly benefit the design work. The following defines the benefits:

- Ensure that the system's expected behavior is captured, documented, and understood by both the business client and the IT project team.
- Define boundaries of the system, what is in scope and what is out of scope.
- Provide a basis for more precise estimation of costs and schedule.
- Establish and maintain agreement with business stakeholders on what the systems should do.

Note that many software development methodologies, like Lean and Agile (see Chap. 9), used in industry place a premium on working features, over written documentation describing the feature. Thus, the relationship between IA and software development is evolving, and each organization has its own flavor of collaboration. Some teams are reducing the amount of written or static documentation and instead substituting working prototypes created by the IA, using software to produce interactive interfaces. *There is no single best solution*, so it is important to choose methods that most effectively communicate with others on the team and help improve efficiency while ensuring the entire user experience is documented, including error states, edge cases, and other conditions.

3.8   Summary

Human centered design includes users, with their needs guiding design and development, while balancing business and technical requirements. IAs and UX designers often lead HCD efforts while serving as the "voice of the user." Iterative design, combining research, design, and evaluation is the best way to produce human-centered products, as it is almost impossible to get the design right the first time. ISO 9241 provides a foundation for HCD, including definitions for the terms usability, effectiveness, efficiency, and satisfaction.

In the following chapters, we will explore the standard's four human-centered design activities:

- Understand and specify the context of use.
- Specify user requirements.
- Produce design solutions to meet these requirements.
- Evaluate the designs against requirements.

The four activities seem so easy, and common sense. Yet, again and again, steps are skipped or user requirements are ignored leading to systems with poor usability, or even systems that are totally abandoned. In an iterative design environment, learning and understanding are built into the process and we design systems with the user in mind, helping to ensure products meet target user needs.

References

Barmer, H., Dzombak, R., Gaston, M., Palat, V., Redner, F., Smith, C., & Smith, T. (2021). *Human-centered AI*. Carnegie Mellon University, Software Engineering Institute.

Buxton, W., & Sniderman, R. (1980). Iteration in the design of the human-computer interface. In *Proceedings of the 13th annual meeting, human factors association of Canada* (pp. 72–81).

Capel, T., & Brereton, M. (2023). What is human-centered about human-centered AI? A map of the research landscape. In *Proceedings of the 2023 CHI conference on human factors in computing systems* (pp. 1–23). https://doi.org/10.1145/3544548.3580959.

Cooper, A. (2004). *The inmates are running the asylum: Why high-tech products drive us crazy and how to restore the sanity*. Sams.

Google Ventures. (2019). *The design sprint*. https://www.gv.com/sprint/.

Hearst, M. A. (2009). *Search user interfaces*. Cambridge University Press.

IDEO. (n.d.). *Design kit: What is human-centered design?* https://www.designkit.org/human-centered-design.html.

International Organization for Standardization. (2019). *Ergonomics of human-system interaction—Part 210: Human-centred design for interactive systems* (ISO Standard No. 9241-210:2019). https://www.iso.org/standard/77520.html.

Meinel, C., & Leifer, L. (Eds.). (2023). *Design thinking research: Innovation—Insight—Then and now*. Springer Nature. https://doi.org/10.1007/978-3-031-36103-6.

Nielsen, J. (1993). Iterative user-interface design. *Computer, 26*(11), 32–41.

Norman, D. (2002). Beyond the computer industry. *Communications of the ACM, 45*(7), 120. https://doi.org/10.1145/514236.514269

Pruitt, J., & Grudin, J. (2003). Personas: Practice and theory. In *Proceedings of the 2003 conference on designing for user experiences* (pp. 1–15). ACM. https://doi.org/10.1145/997078.997089.

Ross, J. (2014). *The business value of user experience*. D3 Infragistics. https://www.infragistics.com/media/335732/the_business_value_of_user_experience-3.pdf.

Shneiderman, B. (2020a). Bridging the gap between ethics and practice: Guidelines for reliable, safe, and trustworthy human-centered AI systems. *ACM Transactions on Interactive Intelligent Systems, 10*(4), 1–31. https://doi.org/10.1145/3419764

Shneiderman, B. (2020b). Human-centered artificial intelligence: Three fresh ideas. *AIS Transactions on Human-Computer Interaction, 12*(3), 109–124. https://doi.org/10.17705/1thci.00131.

Tunkelang, D. (2009). Faceted search. *Synthesis Lectures on Information Concepts, Retrieval, and Services, 1*(1), 1–80. https://doi.org/10.2200/S00190ED1V01Y200904ICR005

Whitten, J. L., & Bentley, L. D. (2007). *Systems analysis and design methods*. McGraw-Hill Education.

Xu, W. (2019). Toward human-centered AI: A perspective from human-computer interaction. *Interactions, 26*(4), 42–46. https://doi.org/10.1145/3328485

Research and Evaluation

Research and evaluation provide the foundation for creating human-centered information spaces. These concepts are all about learning and understanding: We first start learning through research about users' goals and needs, next we design and build attempting to meet those needs, and then finally evaluate to learn how well what we built performs. Research helps to *build the right thing*—the features and tools that users want, and evaluation helps make sure we *build the thing right*—that the thing performs as intended (Hanson, 2013), *where the "thing" is an information system.*

Research informs the initial design and build of a new product, as shown in Fig. 4.1. As the system is used, we evaluate it for performance, and make iterative improvements over time. After each iteration, we again evaluate (thus, the arrow pointing back to evaluate). Finally, as new technologies emerge and the context or environment fundamentally changes we will need to introduce more substantial improvements, and go back into the research stage. Examples of new technology are the launch of the iPhone in 2007, and the introduction of Generative AI technology in 2023–2024.

We think about it like this: Research is learning about user goals and needs, gathering the requirements to build something new, while evaluation is helping to determine how well a design meets those goals and needs. Research and evaluation are sometimes given the labels "generative research" and "evaluative research", or "formative research" and "summative research" and methods are shared between the two. In this chapter we discuss user research and evaluation methods in the context of continuous improvement and iterative human-centered design (HCD).

W. Ding et al., *Information Architecture and UX Design*, Synthesis Lectures on Information Concepts, Retrieval, and Services, https://doi.org/10.1007/978-3-031-72138-0_4

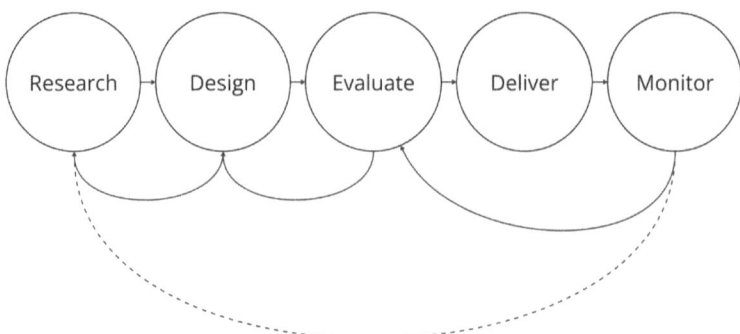

Fig. 4.1   An iterative research and evaluation process

4.1   Research Framework

Any design process requires significant research activities to learn about users and how to meet their needs. Research does the following:

- Collects objective data from users to learn behavior and context.
- Collects relevant facts, best practices, and design principles that help the team formulate and understand an overall design strategy.
- Lays the foundation for strategy and design work.
- Saves time and avoids unnecessary mistakes in design and development parts of the project. Increases the chances for successful adoption by users.
- Increases the chances for successful adoption by users.

Research requires a focus on three areas: context, content, and users (Rosenfeld et al., 2015).

- **Context** research deals with short and long term business goals and technology capabilities/limitations. User Experience (UX) researchers must learn these so they can be matched to user goals and needs.
- **Content** research covers the information (such as text and images) itself, and how it is presented in the system. We must learn who creates and maintains the content and how it is currently organized.
- **User** research collects data about user behaviors, perception, and performance. This can include their environment, culture, and level of experience among other factors.

Outcomes of these research activities can include:

- Clearly stated objectives of the project, including business and user outcomes.
- Product strategy; including recommendations, rationales, and requirements.
- One or more research reports.
- Navigation structures, and user flows (Chap. 3).
- Personas and user journeys.

4.2   Evaluation

Once we've researched, designed, and built a system, evaluation helps us see what we got right and what needs improvement. Evaluation investigates how well the design meets the business goals and user needs. Most importantly, it provides data to drive redesign efforts and continuous improvements. Two of the most popular ways of evaluating systems are usability testing and surveys (Sauro & Lewis, 2016).

4.2.1   The Need for Evaluation

The paper "Evaluating Information Architecture" by Toub (2000), although written many years ago, is still a good starting point, especially for understanding the challenges earlier design professionals faced when most organizations did not conduct evaluations. Toub clearly explains why evaluation is needed, its benefits, and the dangers of not assessing site information architecture including lost revenue, lower productivity, and legal liability.

Compared to the situations described in the paper (no evaluation of IA), design practices have come a long way. More attention is being paid to the overall success of the user experience, organizations have adopted design guidelines, and digital design patterns have emerged. Today, *a good user experience is now seen as a competitive advantage*, and many companies now have dedicated and well-trained research teams dedicated to research and evaluation.

However, as we are all aware, there are still many poorly designed websites and apps or "hallucinating" artificial intelligence (AI) results that end up frustrating the user and causing business losses as well. Why is this the case? Unfortunately, not all companies follow good human-centered design practices. Sometimes organizations feel the need to move quickly, limiting the ability to conduct research. Or, they think they "know what people want." In addition, *people's expectations of usability are getting higher and higher*. When users have good experiences with well-designed websites or apps, they become less tolerant of poor design and they are more likely to reject those that are not up to date to today's usability standards.

4.3   Research and Evaluation Methods

A description of selected user research and evaluation methods is shared in Table 4.1, along with pros and cons. As you will see, there are many methods to choose from. Becoming familiar with these techniques will help you select the best method for your research purposes. Note that some methods can be combined in a single study. For example, very often usability testing and interviews are combined to understand what happened through observation in the usability test, with additional details through an interview that takes place during the same session.

When choosing the right research method or combination of methods, one needs to consider a set of criteria—from the sample size of study participants, nature of data required, and purpose of research—to time and resource constraints. Start with the research questions, what is it that you want to learn? Next, determine time and other constraints or limitations you may have. Then choose the participants and methods that you think will answer the questions. Finally, consider how you will present the results. Every method has its pros and cons, so be sure to carefully consider how you will conduct research to answer your research questions.

4.3.1   Qualitative and Quantitative Data

An important consideration when planning research is to consider what types of data you need to answer your research questions. UX researchers collect two main types of data in their research, quantitative and qualitative. One way to think about quantitative and qualitative is *numbers and words*:

- **Quantitative is numbers**: Shows *what* happened.
  Example: Participant B spent 90 s to find the correct content, versus the target time of 60 s.
- **Qualitative is words:** Explains *why* something happened or user perceptions.
  Example: Participant B reported the navigation is "cluttered and confusing."

Do you see how the two results go together? The research participant spent much more time than the target to complete a task. This by itself is valuable and is made more actionable when combined with qualitative feedback. Given these results—the researcher could recommend simplifying the navigation (perhaps by conducting a card sort and tree test) to help improve efficiency.

For qualitative usability studies, you usually have a relatively smaller number of participants who will give you in-depth responses to interview questions, usability tasks, and similar data. In this type of research, you are looking to identify and fix problems you observe. For example, when illustrating why 5 users is sufficient for a qualitative usability

Table 4.1 Primary UX research and evaluation methods

Research/evaluation method	Best used for
A/B testing	Comparing two or more versions of an system or feature to see which performs better. Often automated through the use of testing software **Pros**: Collects quantitative data to see which design performs better against desired metrics in natural user interaction settings, in a non-intrusive manner **Cons**: Can be difficult to set up, requires specialized software. May take a long time to get significant results
Benchmarking	Comparing performance of the same system at two points in time or assessing the strengths and weaknesses of comparable systems (competitive benchmarking) and looking for gaps or areas for improvement **Pros**: Provides a look at how a system compares to a previous state or its peers **Cons**: Usability and effectiveness of competitor designs may not be known
Card sorting (open and closed)	Testing Information Architecture (IA) structures and studying users' mental models. Open card sorting allows the user to create new categories and terms, in addition to existing. Closed card sorting restricts users to existing categories and terms. Terms used in card sorting can be created based upon results from many other research methods, such as interviews, observations, and search log analysis **Pros**: A powerful tool that can be used both qualitatively and quantitatively **Cons**: Quantitative analysis may need special software. Results need to be presented in a meaningful way
Cognitive walkthrough	Evaluating a system by acting as a persona to complete a task, and compiling issues that are found **Pros**: Usually easy to perform, can provide results quickly **Cons**: Does not involve real users. Must know the persona and task to perform

(continued)

Table 4.1 (continued)

Research/evaluation method	Best used for
Content analysis, mapping, and inventory	Understanding the current content in a system and its structure **Pros**: Provides a full view of the content held by a system or organization **Cons**: Can be time consuming, may ignore context
Contextual inquiry	Understanding users' goals and tasks based on real-life behavior in their natural environment; sometimes called "in the wild," field studies, or ethnography **Pros**: Data gathering takes place in the context of a user's work. Data is more concrete based on in-the-moment experience, and is more objective and natural. May discover unanticipated issues **Cons**: Opportunistic and time-consuming, generating large amounts of data that takes time to analyze
Diary study	Collecting longitudinal user reports that can be used to follow behaviors, goals, and tasks over time **Pros**: Collects detailed data over an extended period of time, in the user's natural environment **Cons**: Can be difficult to set up, high drop out rate among participants
Desirability testing (Benedek & Miner, 2002)	Collecting users' positive, negative, and neutral reactions to a system, by having them choose descriptions from a set of terms provided by the researcher **Pros**: Easy to set up, provides easy to understand visuals **Cons**: May not provide data explaining users' subjective assessments
Expert evaluation	Evaluating systems to identify usability issues using expert knowledge and checklists **Pros**: Usually easy to perform, can provide results quickly **Cons**: Does not involve real users. May be biased by the reviewer's skills and background

(continued)

Table 4.1 (continued)

Research/evaluation method	Best used for
Focus groups	Collecting opinions, ideas and visioning data. Good for high-level starting points and trend data **Pros**: Like a group interview. Can reach multiple people at the same time. Participants may be inspired by each other and provide more valuable opinions and ideas **Cons**: Participant opinions may be influenced by others. Out of context of a task
Heuristic evaluation	Evaluating an information space to identify usability issues. Trained evaluators inspect a system using a checklist of heuristics, noting usability issues and categorizing them on a severity scale **Pros**: Can be completed relatively quickly, does not require recruiting participants. Can provide an ordered list of issues and severity ratings **Cons**: Does not involve real users, and is dependent on the skill and background of the evaluators
Interviews	Gaining an understanding about users' goals, problems, and desires. Within the project team, you can interview stakeholders to understand business objectives **Pros**: Less ambiguity, can ask follow-up questions to probe unexpected topics or clarify issues. Relatively easy to conduct **Cons**: Subjective and retrospective (can be difficult for users to accurately recall past events). Can be time consuming to analyze transcripts
Participatory design	Developing innovative concepts by co-designing with users. Insights are generally gathered in the form of sketches or other low-fidelity designs **Pros**: A picture is worth a thousand words, helps users translate their ideas into visuals, which may be more expressive **Cons**: Users may have differing levels of design interest or expressiveness. Be careful to remember the user is giving ideas, not a final design to follow

(continued)

Table 4.1 (continued)

Research/evaluation method	Best used for
Surveys	Collecting preferences and opinions from one or many large groups through written questionnaires **Pros**: Able to reach many people **Cons**: Low response rate. Ambiguity in question and/or answer (no clarification). Subjective (self-reporting) and retrospective (subject to error)
Task analysis	Understanding users' activities and cognitive processes needed to complete tasks. Hierarchical task analysis (HTA) is a common method used to decompose high-level tasks into a hierarchy of sub-tasks **Pros**: Identifies what tasks should be considered and supported in a design; what works well and what needs improvement in existing flows **Cons**: Difficult to determine impact of iterative design/development on identified tasks. Can be time consuming
Tree testing	Understanding the performance of a navigation system by observing users' click paths to find information. This is like a reverse card sort **Pros**: Can identify issues with navigation paths **Cons**: Does not test the usability of the final navigation design (e.g. mega menus, dropdowns)
Usability testing (in-person and remote)	Identifying design defects in a system. Usually combined with an interview for clarification and follow-up. Can be conducted in-person or remote, and may be moderated or unmoderated (using specialized software). Techniques like "think aloud," and eye-tracking can be used during the test **Pros**: Rich data both verbal and behavioral. Systems being tested can be low or high fidelity **Cons**: Lab setting and artificial tasks may decrease the value of the data. May be hard to include a large number of participants, although this can be mitigated with remote testing
Usage statistics, log analysis, technical/Customer support records	Identifying usage patterns and finding problems that need more investigation. Use technical support/call center logs to identify common user problems **Pros**: Data is objective and rich. May discover in-depth information about user flows **Cons**: Sheer volume of data. May need special software to collect and analyze data

test, Budiu (2021) explains: "If one person falls into a pothole, you know you need to fix it. You don't need 100 people to fall into it to decide it needs fixing." Compare this to quantitative studies where statistically significant results are needed, you may need to calculate the sample size, margin of error, and confidence level, and more. Examples of quantitative studies include surveys and A/B testing in a live system, and they generally require many more participants.

To further illustrate quantitative and qualitative, below we share an example from our IA practice of examining a low performing shopping cart in e-Commerce. In this scenario, a team had quantitative data—the number of people who put an item in the cart and the number of completed purchases (called conversion rate). What they needed was qualitative data to add understanding to solve the problem, and the answer was surprising at the time.

4.3.2 e-Commerce Shopping Cart Example

From the business point of view a shopping cart on e-Commerce sites is where people place things for purchase. In this case, log analysis showed a lot of people were adding items and not completing a purchase—the numbers just did not add up. Thus, a conclusion was drawn that the shopping cart was broken and a big redesign was needed. However, usability research discovered the shopping cart was working just as expected... by the users! The design was functioning properly, but in fact the cart had many uses. Findings included:

- Carts can be used as a place to save items for later review, and
- Carts can be a place to calculate the final cost including shipping and taxes before deciding if the final total is acceptable.

Once these behaviors were discovered (neither of which involve completing a purchase), additional website features were designed. Today, in e-Commerce we often see a "wish list" feature and shipping charges clearly displayed with products. *Log analysis in this instance provided quantitative data* identifying a problem, but not why it was occurring. Following up with *qualitative research provided the why* and suggested that expanded features were needed. The point is to not just discover what is happening; you must also try to understand why it occurs—the answers may surprise you.

4.3.3 Research Standards

With so many methods available, it's good to have a head-start when initiating a research project. Whenever possible, re-use published, validated, research techniques, methods, and surveys—remember the saying *good artists borrow, great artists steal*. Except here we're

Table 4.2 Heuristics from: https://www.nngroup.com/articles/ten-usability-heuristics

1. Visibility of system status	6. Recognition rather than recall
2. Match between system and the real world	7. Flexibility and efficiency of use
	8. Aesthetic and minimalist design
3. User control and freedom	9. Help users recognize, diagnose, and recover from errors
4. Consistency and standards	
5. Error prevention	10. Help and documentation

not stealing, we're doing the right thing by using best-in class methods which are freely shared in the UX community. Let's take a look at some of the more common methods.

4.3.4 Heuristic Evaluation

Heuristic evaluation (Nielsen & Molich, 1990) is a *discount usability technique* that allows design professionals to identify design problems against a formal or informal set of design guidelines called heuristics. In a heuristic review, trained evaluators examine a system and note usability flaws, classifying them using the list of heuristics and rating their severity from cosmetic to critical. After each evaluator rates the system individually, they meet and discuss their findings. Expert reviews and cognitive walkthroughs are similar to heuristic reviews in that they involve researchers looking at a system through the eyes of a user. Table 4.2 reproduces the classic list of ten heuristics that form the foundation of many heuristic evaluations.

4.3.5 Card Sorting

Card sorting explores how users naturally group items together. Participants in these studies are given cards with terms on them that they pile together into categories. There are two types of card sorting. In an open card sort, users place the cards together in piles they create and name each pile as a new category. Categories are not predefined and users can create their own names for them. This is a good way to learn about how users naturally group content. In a closed sort, users place the cards into predefined categories. This is a good way to see if content fits well into the categories previously created. The two can be combined, conducting an open card sort to identify categories, then a closed card sort to see how well the categories work. Card sorting can be analyzed using specialized software that gives us the groupings in chart called a dendogram, providing a compelling visual result.

Card sorting is a relatively easy way to gather qualitative data about the organization of an information space. Using online tools, IAs can collect data and run analysis in an efficient manner with dozens of participants. Tree testing is the natural follow up to card sorting and is used to evaluate the developed navigation structures.

4.3.6 Usability Testing

Usability testing evaluates an information system by investigating its performance with real users. Testing may include prototypes (early, unfinished versions of the system— even paper prototypes) to help guide design and development, or the final product to see how well it works. During a usability test, IAs identify usability problems and collect data related to effectiveness, efficiency, and satisfaction (remember the ISO definition of usability from Chap. 3). Findings from the study can be compared to benchmarks or goals and used to prioritize design strategies.

In a usability test, researchers typically learn:

- Are users successful when completing tasks?
- What paths and workflows do people use to complete tasks?
- How long do tasks take to complete?
- How satisfied are users with the system?
- Recommendations for design changes and improvements.

Usability testing can be conducted in-person in a lab setting, remotely through online conferencing tools like Zoom, or by using specialized research software. Sessions should be run often, each with a relatively modest number of participants depending on the research need (Nielsen, 1995). Usability tests are often combined with interviews, so the IA can learn more by asking about user behaviors observed during the session.

4.3.7 Surveys and System Usability Scale (SUS)

Surveys are questionnaires sent to selected users to gather feedback from the questions they answer. Closed-questions and open-ended questions are usually included. A closed question is one where the user has to choose from predefined answers, while an open-ended question allows the user to write their own response. Closed questions allow for quantitative analysis, while open-ended questions gather qualitative data.

Fig. 4.2 SUS score reporting over a series of benchmarking studies on a website. 68 is the SUS average score across hundreds of sites. When do you think the redesign happened?

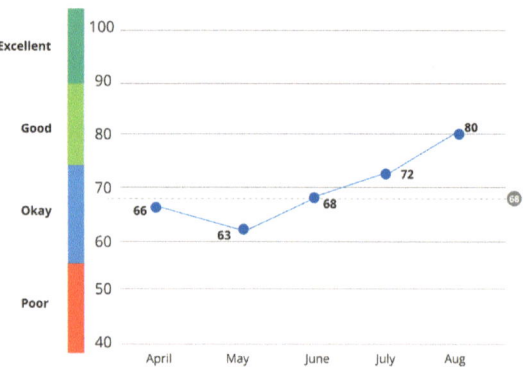

IAs should keep their surveys as short as possible while still collecting the required data. Doing so will increase the completion rate. Many survey tools are available online, providing options to reach wider audiences and making it more convenient for respondents. With any survey, validating questions before launching the study is necessary, which is where standardized questionnaires can be a huge boost to the researcher.

Standardized questionnaires like the System Usability Scale, (Brooke, 2013) gives us a valid and reliable way to assess the perceived usability of a system. Because the 10 question SUS has been used so many times across industries, we can benchmark results for our system against others in a public database, using letter grades or a poor to excellent rating, and against our previous score over time (Fig. 4.2). The more recent Usability Metric for User Experience (UMUX) and UMUX-Lite questionnaires are slimmed down from the SUS 10 questions and provide similarly useful usability scores. (Lewis et al., 2013). The website MeasuringU has a wealth of useful material on SUS and similar usability questionnaires, https://measuringu.com/category/sus/.

4.3.8 Observation and Contextual Inquiry

In observation and contextual inquiry, researchers view users in a naturalistic setting, like their home or office, as they perform real work not tasks created for the research study. Sometimes this is called "in the wild," because the researcher leaves their workplace and travels to the user. Observation is excellent for getting a view of how users interact with integrated information spaces, without the constraints of a usability test.

Being observed is unnatural to many people and can influence behavior. To put the participant at ease it is sometimes recommended that sessions be structured in an expert and novice format, where the IA takes on the role of new employee learning how to do a job. Data collected in contextual inquiries often includes findings that would be impossible to collect with any other method, like observing printed instructions on a user's desk, seeing how they would contact a colleague for assistance, or noting how often they are interrupted in their workflow.

4.3.9 Interviews

During an interview, the researcher talks with an individual user face to face, over the phone, or via online channels. Before the session, IAs should write up a list of questions and follow-up probes, called a protocol. Sessions are usually recorded and transcribed, either in part or in full and then coded to identify themes across many sessions—user quotes are the data to be analyzed. Interviews are excellent for getting each participant's point of view, without influence from others as might happen in a group setting. This technique can stand on its own, or be combined with other methods, to capture qualitative data that supplement quantitative findings.

4.3.10 Usage Statistics and Log Analysis

Logs record user activity in a system and provide an abundance of information about how people use systems and where they run into problems in real-world use. The quantitative nature of the log data can empower researchers to very effectively communicate ideas to business stakeholders. The following are metrics (Table 4.3) often used for website analysis.

Additionally, search logs can be used to get valuable insights. If logs show search is the most important feature of a site, that does not necessarily mean users are search dominant. Instead, it may mean the navigation is insufficient. Terms drawn from search logs are often used to improve site labeling and navigation structures. Metrics extracted from search logs include:

Table 4.3 Site level and page level metrics

Site level metrics	Page level metrics
• Total site visits • Total unique visitors • Count of each site page visits • Average time spent per visit • Referring pages: the top channels used to get to the site	• Visits/unique visitors to page • Total page views • Visits to page as entry page • Visits to page as exit page • Average time spent on page • Bounce rate • Clickstream

- Top queries over a timeframe, like 3 months prior.
- Search terms with no results.
- The percentage of search results that users click on, called Click-Through Rate (CTR).
- Sessions: The series of searches performed by a user in a single session.
- Time to First Click: How long it takes for users to click on a result after performing a search.
- Query Reformulation Rate: The frequency with which users modify their queries.
- Success Rate: The percentage of searches that result in users finding the information they need.

4.4   Research Deliverables

In addition to comprehensive research reports combining quantitative and qualitative data, personas and journeys are a way to share findings in an engaging and accessible format. User personas are fictional characters created to represent different user types that are based on the research. In other words, user personas are created via research, and consolidate and communicate the data into a representation of a user type. User Journeys show the steps people take to complete a task or reach a goal. Along with the stages of a journey, user emotions, challenges, and opportunities are typically shown.

4.4.1   User Personas

User personas are fictional characters created to represent different user types that are based on the research. In other words, user personas are created via research, and consolidate and communicate the data into a representation of a user type. A persona has personal identifiers like a name, demographics, motivations, and goals. The persona concept was first introduced to the user interface design field by Cooper (2004) and can help IAs stay focused on the user, avoid designing for one's self, and avoid designing for needs that don't really exist.

4.4.2   Use of Personas

There are different practices in using personas:

- Using personas to create a rigorous form of user model, based on behavioral patterns that emerge from observational research. Personas can be used to represent the key behaviors, attitudes, skill levels, goals, work, and environment of real people. Personas also lay the foundation on which to build user flows and scenarios. The two are then used to guide the system's functionality and design.

- Conducting quantitative analysis based on personas to determine and prioritize system/product features to be built. Pruitt and Grudin (2003) use "persona-weighted feature matrix" to help the development team to determine what features and capabilities the system should have.
- Using personas as a medium for communication. As described by Pruitt and Grudin (2003), while comprehensive user research reports provide valuable insights into design, many team members may not actually read them or end up remembering very little about them. When the results are represented by personas, team members are engaged more effectively. Personas utilize the power of narrative and storytelling to enhance attention, memory, and organization of detailed user data.
- Using personas is best when it is impossible to list exhaustively all the user types and characteristics. When there is a possibility to get complete statistics about users, a comprehensive user profiling approach might be more appropriate.

4.4.3 Benefits of Personas

A persona is both a design tool and a communication tool. Its main benefits include the following:

- Help team members share a specific, consistent understanding of various audience groups.
- Features or functions can be prioritized based on how well they address the needs of one or more personas.
- Provide a human "face" so as to focus empathy on the persons represented by the demographics.
- Create a good container to hold research data.

4.4.4 Personas Construction

Constructing personas is a dedicated process. Special attention is needed to the following:

- Build personas around identified goals and behaviors based on the data. If rich data is not available, "proto-personas" based on assumptions may be considered, but do not confuse these with genuine personas.
- Determine how much information can be fictional (like name or location) while still having the persona based on real data.

Fig. 4.3 Framework for a basic persona

- Avoid resume-like personas. Do not use separate personas with less data for communication with other teams, and a more comprehensive persona document for IAs and designers.
- Consider the persona and user journey together, to give a full picture of the user and their experience (Fig. 4.3).

4.4.5   User Journeys

User journeys go hand in hand with personas. And like personas, they use the research you've conducted to help build a real-world view of the user experience. Journeys show the high-level steps users take to accomplish a goal, often using multiple channels, and may take place over days, weeks, or months as compared to user flows (Chap. 3) that take place in a single session. They include multiple touchpoints and aim to demonstrate the user's actions, emotions, and challenges. Journey deliverables (Fig. 4.4) include sections for the researcher to point out where problems are encountered, often called pain points, and recommendations to improve. They are especially useful for showing how different technologies, people, and products interact over time.

4.4.6   Benefits of User Journeys

User journeys share many of the same benefits of personas. A journey communicates a multi-step process in an straightforward visual. Its main benefits include the following:

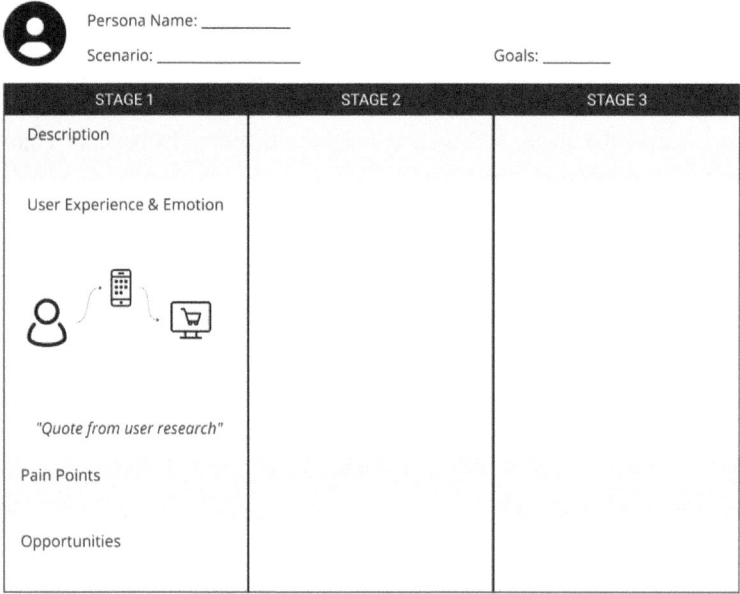

Fig. 4.4 Framework for a basic user journey

- Clearly shows the stages of a journey, different technologies or systems used, and outcomes.
- Lists pain points or frustrations in each stage, the challenges blocking the user from making progress.
- Gives researchers a place to suggest opportunities for improvement.
- A good container to hold research data.

4.4.7   User Journey Construction

Constructing journeys is similar to personas. Use the data collected to create journeys focused on user goals, behaviors, and outcomes based on the data. Include the data—like user quotes—to make the journeys very powerful. Business stakeholders like to see the data, and this is a chance to make it accessible.

The anatomy of a user journey includes:

- Header
    - Persona name: Who is the persona taking the journey?
    - Scenario: Describe the context of the journey.
    - Goals: The outcomes our persona wants or needs

- Main body
  - Stages: Find natural breaks in the journey and name each stage from start to finish.
  - Description: Give some context for each stage, what are the activities and outcomes?
  - User Experience & Emotion: Use text, images, and icons to communicate the user's experience in the stage, and their emotional reactions. Draw lines connecting the different activities and interactions.
  - Quotes from user research: Share quotes (or other data) to heighten the impact of the journey and demonstrate the data you've used to inform the deliverable.
  - Pain Points: The frustrations and challenges experienced by the persona.
  - Opportunities: Actions the team can take to improve the user experience and outcomes.

Consider delivering personas and user journeys together as a package. Take care to find the right balance of complexity in your work. Too complex and it will be unusable, too simple and it won't inform. When in doubt, we've found it better to err towards the more simple and understandable.

4.5   Research for AI

AI research can be seen through two lenses, intrinsic and extrinsic evaluation (Resnik & Lin, 2010), and together they can give a *holistic* (Liang et al., 2022) view of AI, like large-language models (LLMs). *Intrinsic* assesses the quality of the AI models themselves and is the domain of data scientists and machine learning experts. *Extrinsic* AI evaluation, on the other hand, is concerned with the impact or contribution of AI as part of a larger system and is where UX researchers can get involved. Abbasian et al. (2024) concisely explain intrinsic and extrinsic:

- "Intrinsic evaluation metrics measure the proficiency of a language model in generating coherent and meaningful sentences relying on language rules and patterns" (Intrinsic evaluation metrics section).
- "Extrinsic evaluation metrics present means of measuring the performance of language models by incorporating user perspectives and real-world contexts" (Extrinsic evaluation metrics section).

In many ways, extrinsic evaluation is the same as any other user research project, with metrics used to assess how the system impacts users and meet needs and goals (Chang et al., 2024). Some examples include, how does an AI powered query analyzer work as part of a search system, and how useful are Generative AI suggestions in a word processing tool. General purpose evaluation metrics for LLMs include: Accuracy; Bias; Calibration; Groundedness; Helpfulness; Safety, Sensibility, Specificity, Interestingness (SSI); Toxicity; Trustfulness; and Usefulness (Abbasian et al., 2024). As AI becomes increasingly a part of our lives and society, human-centered research and evaluation using metrics like those above will become even more important.

Researchers in AI applications can also use metrics, like Google's (2023) business impact metrics, which are similar to web and search usage statistics, as a starting point for evaluating AI systems:

- Adoption rate: Percentage of active users divided by the total intended audience.
- Frequency of use: Daily, weekly, and monthly queries.
- Session length: Average length of continuous user interactions
- Queries per session: Average number of queries submitted per session.
- Query length: Average number of words or characters per query.
- Abandonment rate: Number and percentage of sessions ended before users are successful.
- User satisfaction: Track user experience and customer satisfaction metrics, such as Net Promoter Score (NPS) and System Usability Scale (SUS).

4.6   AI for Research

Just as it is evolving *what* we research, AI is also changing *how* we research—providing capabilities to support design iterations and testing. Although research methods themselves have remained relatively unchanged—AI tools can make things faster, more efficient, and provide new channels for research, design and evaluation. Lu et al. (2022) identified four areas that can be supported by AI:

- Design inspiration: Including guidelines and best practices.
- Design alternatives: AI to generate multiple designs for exploration.
- Design customization: Adapting customized widgets automatically.
- Guideline violations: Comparing designs against accessibility and usability guidelines. By incorporating AI in these areas, researchers and designers should see improvements, with the capabilities improving rapidly.

AI tools, while still imperfect, are being adopted by practitioners—a survey of 1093 researchers found that 77.1% have used AI in some fashion for their work (User Interviews, 2022). This finding includes popular research tools like Dovetail or HotJar that incorporate some AI elements, and dedicated AI like ChatGPT.

In addition to evaluating the designs, AI can greatly improve the efficiency of a research practice. For example, until recently many interviews and usability sessions were conducted face-to-face in a usability lab and required travel, coordination, and substantial expense. Compare this to today, where sessions are automatically scheduled using online calendars, like Calendly (https://calendly.com/) and videoconferencing like Zoom (https://

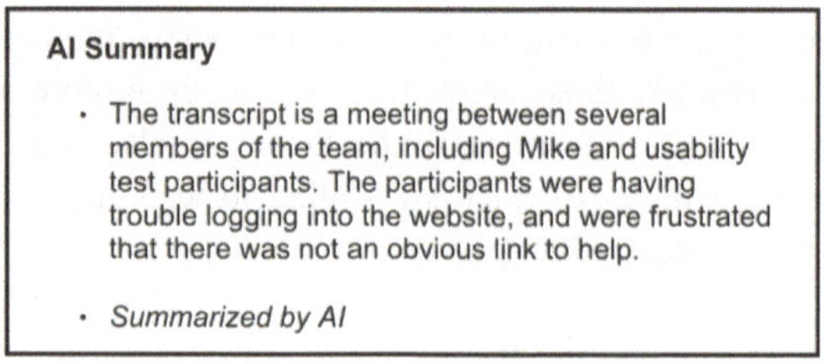

Fig. 4.5 AI summarization of
a recorded user interview in a
user research tool

AI Summary

· The transcript is a meeting between several
  members of the team, including Mike and usability
  test participants. The participants were having
  trouble logging into the website, and were frustrated
  that there was not an obvious link to help.

· *Summarized by AI*

Fig. 4.6 AI powered interview
transcription and sentiment
analysis in a user research tool.
Notice Yes/No to give
feedback on the accuracy

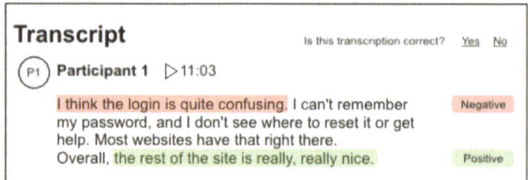

Transcript   Is this transcription correct? Yes No

P1 Participant 1   ▷11:03

I think the login is quite confusing, I can't remember   Negative
my password, and I don't see where to reset it or get
help. Most websites have that right there.
Overall, the rest of the site is really, really nice.   Positive

zoom.us/) is used to virtually host and record the meeting. Another great example of AI in research is transcribing, summarizing, and coding interview recordings (Figs. 4.5 and 4.6). In the authors' experience (and many others) each hour of interview time took about three to four hours to manually transcribe, and sometimes even more depending on the topic and number of speakers. In a business environment, this meant that *researchers were often under time pressure and the work was not always in sync* with other parts of a project.

Compare this to today, where the interview is recorded and uploaded to an AI powered transcribing tool. In minutes a text transcription is completed and a summary provided. We have a pretty good picture of the results and the researcher can then go through and code to find more themes, and look in-depth where needed. While AI may not yet meet the accuracy of humans (Pentland et al., 2023), tools support quick corrections meaning AI and automations save hours freeing researchers to focus on other tasks and critically *helping keep research in sync with fast paced projects.*

4.7   Summary

Research and evaluation is an important part of designing systems that meet user needs and ensure optimal performance. There are many UX research methods, and it is essential to understand the pros and cons and select the right ones to answer your research questions. UX research enhances the usability of systems, including those with AI features, and advances in AI provide researchers with new tools to improve data collection and analysis. The end goal of any research is to provide teams with the critical data needed to create outstanding interfaces.

References

Abbasian, M., Khatibi, E., Azimi, I., Oniani, D., Shakeri Hossein Abad, Z., Thieme, A., Sriram, R., Yang, Z., Wang, Y., Lin, B., Gevaert, O., Li, L. J., Jain, R., & Rahmani, A. M. (2024). Foundation metrics for evaluating effectiveness of healthcare conversations powered by generative AI. *NPJ Digital Medicine, 7*(1), 82. https://doi.org/10.1038/s41746-024-01074-z.

Benedek, J., & Miner, T. (2002). Measuring desirability: New methods for evaluating desirability in a usability lab setting. *Proceedings of Usability Professionals Association, 2003,* 8–12.

Blandford, A., Furniss, D., & Makri, S. (2016). Qualitative HCI research: Going behind the scenes. *Synthesis Lectures on Human-Centered Informatics, 9*(1), 1–115.

Brooke, J. (2013). SUS: A retrospective JUS. *Journal of Usability Studies, 8*(2), 29–40.

Budiu, R. (2021). *Why 5 participants are okay in a qualitative study, but not in a quantitative one.* NNGroup. https://www.nngroup.com/articles/5-test-users-qual-quant/.

Chang, Y., Wang, X., Wang, J., Wu, Y., Yang, L., Zhu, K., Chen, H., Yi, X., Wang, C., Wang, Y., Ye, W., & Xie, X. (2024). A survey on evaluation of large language models. *ACM Transactions on Intelligent Systems and Technology, 15*(3), 1–45.

Cooper, A. (2004). *The inmates are running the asylum: Why high-tech products drive us crazy and how to restore the sanity.* Sams.

Google. (2023). *KPIs for gen AI: Why measuring your new AI is essential to its success.* https://cloud.google.com/transform/kpis-for-gen-ai-why-measuring-your-new-ai-is-essential-to-its-success.

Hanson, N. (2013). *Humanizing business technology.* http://www.slideshare.net/ndhanthro/humanizing-business-technology.

Lewis, J. R., Utesch, B. S., & Maher, D. E. (2013). UMUX-LITE: When there's no time for the SUS. In *Proceedings of the SIGCHI conference on human factors in computing systems* (pp. 2099–2102). https://doi.org/10.1145/2470654.2481287.

Lewis, J. R., & Sauro, J. (2021). Usability and user experience: Design and evaluation. In G. Salvendy & W. Karwowski (Eds.), *Handbook of human factors and ergonomics* (pp. 8972–1015). https://doi.org/10.1002/9781119636113.ch3.

Liang, P., Bommasani, R., Lee, T., Tsipras, D., Soylu, D., Yasunaga, M., Zhang, Y., Narayanan, D., Wu, Y., Kumar, A., Newman, B., & Koreeda, Y. (2022). *Holistic evaluation of language models.* arXiv preprint arXiv:2211.09110.

Lu, Y., Zhang, C., Zhang, I., & Li, T. J. J. (2022). Bridging the Gap between UX practitioners' work practices and AI-enabled design support tools. In *CHI conference on human factors in computing systems extended abstracts* (pp. 1–7). https://doi.org/10.1145/3491101.3519809.

Methodology, 26(6), 661–677. https://doi.org/10.1080/13645579.2022.2087849.

Nielsen, J., & Molich, R. (1990). Heuristic evaluation of user interfaces. In *Proceedings of the SIGCHI conference on human factors in computing systems* (pp. 249–256).

Nielsen, J. (1995). *10 Heuristics for user interface design.* Retrieved December 24, 2016, from https://www.nngroup.com/articles/ten-usability-heuristics/.

Pentland, S. J., Fuller, C. M., Spitzley, L. A., & Twitchell, D. P. (2023). Does accuracy matter? Methodological considerations when using automated speech-to-text for social science research. *International Journal of Social Research Methodology, 26*(6), 661–677.

Pruitt, J., & Grudin, J. (2003). Personas: Practice and theory. In *Proceedings of the 2003 conference on designing for user experiences* (pp. 1–15). ACM. https://doi.org/10.1145/997078.997089.

Resnik, P., & Lin, J. (2010). *Evaluation of NLP systems. The handbook of computational linguistics and natural language processing* (pp. 271–295).

Rosenfeld, L., Morville, P., & Arango, J. (2015). *Information architecture* (4th ed.). O'Reilly Media.

Sauro, J, & Lewis, J. R. (2016). *Quantifying the user experience* (2nd ed.). Morgan Kaufmann.

Toub, S. (2000). *Evaluating information architecture: A practical guide to assessing web site organization.* Argus Center for Information Architecture.

Information Organization and Navigation Design

Information architects (IAs) and UX designers spend a lot of time planning and designing organization and navigation systems. The ways people interact and navigate a website, app, or other information space greatly depends on semantic organization, controlled vocabularies/taxonomies, content organization and relationships, and what kinds of navigation systems are implemented. Looking back to the Generative Generation from chapter two, we see here tagging and AI agents that reflect the evolution of information systems over time, from one of read-only top-down control, to one that supports bottom-up organization and on-the-fly content creation. In this chapter, we discuss organization and navigation systems together as they are closely related to each other.

To learn about organization and navigation systems, the first thing an IA should do is become familiar with the prevailing methods and techniques—many of which come from the library and information sciences.

In general, to have good information architecture, one needs to consider the following components:

- Logical Organization
  e.g., alphabetic, numerical, and hierarchical organization schemas as well as placement and labels
- Semantic Organization
  e.g., metadata, controlled vocabularies, content indexing, and tagging
- Structural Navigation
  e.g., global, local and contextual navigation, process/wizard navigation, and browsing aids

W. Ding et al., *Information Architecture and UX Design*, Synthesis Lectures on Information Concepts, Retrieval, and Services, https://doi.org/10.1007/978-3-031-72138-0_5

- Search
  e.g., search algorithms, search result displays, search interfaces, AI agents, and other search aids

Each of the components will be discussed below.

5.1   Logical Organization

One of our favorite references on organization systems is Kipfer's (1997)"*The Order of Things: How Everything in the World is Organized …into Hierarchies, Structures, and Pecking Order.*" Kipfer provides ample examples of "naturally organized" structures for things ranging from the smallest to the size of the universe, showing that orders exist in nature and in our civilization. If we can identify the appropriate order and organize our knowledge accordingly, we can make every subject easier to understand and follow.

An important, yet often overlooked organization method is to identify and make use of the natural order: No matter the type of information spaces and subject area, there are certain order systems that appear natural and are easy for the user to follow. Common natural or logical order systems are shown in Table 5.1.

All these methods have an *order* that can be defined systematically. For information organization, IAs need to decide which of these methods to implement and let users understand how it was used to organize the content and the display, so they may easily find what they want. Figure 5.1 shows a list of graduate programs sorted alphabetically helping the user scan and find. Imagine this list, or one much longer, that is not logically ordered. How hard would it be to find the information you want?

In e-commerce users often sort large collections of products, as shown in Fig. 5.2. While the default is Top Sellers, shoppers can change the order in which products are shown to enhance findability. This sorting uses logical ordering, like alphabetical (brand), numerical (price), or time (new arrivals). Imagine a scenario where shoppers are looking for an item made by the brand "Adidas." They could sort by Brand, and easily see Adidas early in the list of products.

5.2   Semantic Organization

Organizing by content is to organize by *semantic relationships* of the content—that is to organize it by its meaning. Semantic organization is one of the most important organization methods for information architecture and has its own descriptive languages and methods. Following, we discuss four major methods of semantic organization: Metadata, controlled vocabulary, faceted classification, and tagging.

Table 5.1 Common natural/logical ordering systems

Ordering system	Example
Alphabetical: ordered by letter, A–Z	Staff directory, department directory
Numerical: ordered by number, 1–100	Items sorted by price, distance, size, or other quantitative attributes
Chronological: ordered by date	Time-sensitive resources such as news articles sorted by date
Geographical: ordered by location	Maps, distance
By tasks: ordered by goal	User goals or needs
Audience: ordered by group	A university website is organized by audience types—faculty, current students, prospective students, and alumni
Metaphor	Rainbows of colors, solar systems, and other things that have apparent natural order
Popularity or usage frequency	Instead of being based on predetermined order, the sequence changes dynamically based on usage or participation such as most-popular, highest rated, or frequently visited
Relevance: ordered by a ranking algorithm	It depends on the way the relevance is calculated, it can be based on a combination of several of the above methods
Personalization and customization	Based on personal preferences or user settings

Graduate Programs
- Master of Science in Data Science
- Master of Science in Health Informatics
- Master of Science in Information - Library and Information Science
- Master of Science in Information - Human-Computer Interaction & User Experience
- Master of Science in Information Systems
- PhD in Information Science

Fig. 5.1 A list of graduate programs. Notice how the organization is alphabetical, making the list easily scannable

5.2.1 Metadata

Metadata is "the information we create, store, and share to describe things, allows us to interact with these things to obtain the knowledge we need" (Riley, 2017, p. 1). Developing metadata is often the first step to getting information organized. Metadata describes digital objects in term of its content, context, and structure (Gilliland-Swetland et al., 2000):

Fig. 5.2 Sorting options often seen in e-commerce. Users may personalize the organization by selecting different items in the menu. The set of results remains the same, only the ordering changes when a new selection is made

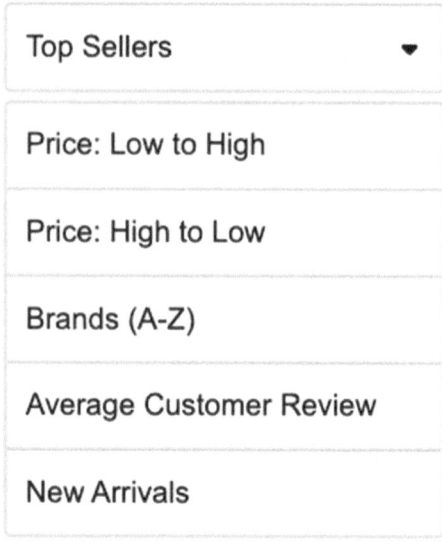

- **Content**: What the object contains or is about.
- **Context**: Who, what, why, where, and how of the object creation.
- **Structure**: Formal associations within or between objects.

The key to helping understand this topic, we've found as teachers, is for our students to not overthink when starting out. It is very easy to get caught up with advanced theories and concepts when first learning about metadata. In fact, metadata can be something as simple as "createdDate = 01/01/2001." However, to make metadata useful we need to take a systematic approach, starting with looking at the kinds of metadata IAs use. Riley (2017) describes the main types of metadata:

- **Descriptive metadata**: Describes an information resource, e.g., title = Drexel University.
- **Structural metadata**: Describes the types, versions, and relationships of information object, e.g., section = 1, chapter = 5, page = 3.
- **Administrative metadata**: Gives technical and other information to help manage the information resource, e.g., source = documentScanner123.
- **Markup languages**: Combines metadata and content together to show notable features, e.g., noting that word is a place name.

Along with its different types, metadata has many important characteristics. These characteristics help make metadata useful and easy to create, maintain, and understand. For IAs, two should be emphasized in particular: Standardization and indexing quality.

5.2.2 Standardization

Standardization means the creators and users of metadata agree to use a shared set of elements. A common metadata standard, Dublin Core Metadata Set ("The Dublin Core" or "DC") defines 15 metadata elements (Table 5.2) that can be used to describe many types of information resources. As simple as they may look, these elements provide a much-needed structure. Everyone who uses DC agrees to abide by the rules of the standard, which lets other people and computers understand use, and share metadata, making information resources easier to manage and extend.

Standardization supports an important feature of metadata, that it is readable by humans and "readable" by computer. Using DC (or other standards), an IA provides metadata that can be processed by computers because the data is in a format computer programs are developed to interpret. For example, with the "language" element, an IA can assign English (en), so that a computer system can deliver only webpages that have the metadata "<html lang = "en-US">" in their metadata for a request from United States. Or, for a Spanish page, the language can be detected and the user given a control to translate to other languages (Fig. 5.3).

Table 5.2 Dublin core elements, https://www.dublincore.org/specifications/dublin-core/dcmi-terms/#section-3

DC elements	Definitions
Contributor	An entity responsible for making contributions to the resource
Coverage	The spatial or temporal topic of the resource, the spatial applicability of the resource, or the jurisdiction under which the resource is relevant
Creator	An entity primarily responsible for making the resource
Date	A point or period of time associated with an event in the lifecycle of the resource
Description	An account of the resource
Format	The file format, physical medium, or dimensions of the resource
Identifier	An unambiguous reference to the resource within a given context
Language	A language of the resource
Publisher	An entity responsible for making the resource available
Relation	A related resource
Rights	Information about rights held in and over the resource
Source	A related resource from which the described resource is derived
Subject	The topic of the resource
Title	A name given to the resource
Type	The nature or genre of the resource

Fig. 5.3 A common
translation feature powered by
the metadata language field

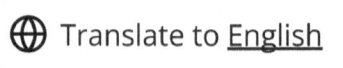

Making these standards findable and publicly accessible is critical. Dublin Core is available on the DC website and was published as ISO standard 15836 (2017). Many other leading information organizations maintain metadata standards for their specific topic areas. The Library of Congress also publishes several important library metadata standards, including PREMIS, METS, and MODS available at https://www.loc.gov/standards/.

5.2.3   Indexing Quality

The second function of metadata is to improve the quality of indexing, which is very important when making resources available through search. Recall that the metadata definition includes making the resource easier to find and retrieve. One easy way to support quality is to use standards like we discussed above.

Training, establishing guidelines, and auditing are all additional techniques we use to help ensure quality. However, they can be time-consuming manual processes. To help in this regard, content management systems and artificial intelligence are being utilized with the goal of improving speed, while maintaining quality. However, a bottleneck of metadata application is still the difficulty in generating it automatically. While a lot of progress has been made for automatic metadata creation, much is still created through a manual process. Content management systems help generate and manage metadata as part of the content creation process, lessening the effort in some cases. AI generated metadata and its use in different domains (e.g., healthcare, humanities) and is an ongoing research area (Tsay et al., 2020; Wu et al., 2015, 2023). In February 2024 ExLibris, a large library automation company, announced its AI powered metadata augmentation tool (ExLibris, 2024), and more are sure to follow. This is an ongoing and active area of research, that is sure to be enhanced by Generative AI.

5.3   Controlled Vocabularies

Other than standard elements, metadata systems have no specific structure. Domain specific structure can be added through controlled vocabularies, which describe the terms to be used in a knowledge domain, called *descriptors*. A descriptor is a unique term assigned to one, and only one, concept in the domain. This means a term that can only be used one time in a vocabulary.

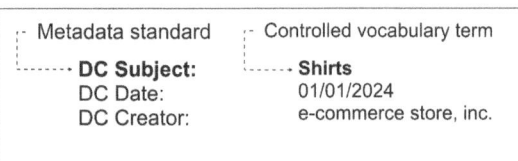

Fig. 5.4 Element from a metadata standard (left), and the value from a controlled vocabulary (right). Only values that are in the controlled vocabulary can be assigned to an element

Controlled vocabularies are terms selected and organized by domain experts to represent concepts in a specific domain of knowledge following general guidelines. Every concept covered within the domain will be assigned a unique term (called descriptor, subject term or preferred term). Other terms with similar meanings will be called equivalent terms, lead-in terms, or synonyms. The relationships between descriptors are established through hierarchical relationships such as Broader Term (BT) and Narrower Term (NT), and associative relationships such as Related Term (RT). Let's look at an example from e-commerce:

5.3.1   Descriptor: Shirts

- Broader Term (BT): Clothing
- Narrower Terms (NT): T-Shirts, Dress Shirts, Casual Shirts
- Related Terms (RT): Tops, Blouses

Using the example above, an e-commerce search engine could find or suggest items for a user's search, even if the keywords do not exactly match the descriptor. A search for "tops" could return products categorized as "shirts." If you've ever searched or browsed an eCommerce site, you've interacted with a controlled vocabulary.

Controlled vocabularies establish a precise mapping between a term/label and a concept, reducing ambiguity caused by homographs, synonyms, polysemes and other problems existing in natural languages. Once controlled vocabularies are created, entries in them can be used as subject terms to index resources (Fig. 5.4).

5.3.2   Advantages of Controlled Vocabularies

There are several advantages of using controlled vocabularies with metadata:

- The content will be represented more precisely and consistently through the carefully selected terms.

- Indexing and searching precision are greatly improved through the terms and relationship structures inherent in controlled vocabularies, facilitating efficient information retrieval.
- Interoperability between systems is supported through a common terminology.
- Term relationships established in the controlled vocabularies add an additional content-based navigation structure like hierarchies, which are very helpful for users' browsing activities.

The disadvantages are the labor-intensive creation process, and the difficulty to maintain and update the vocabularies to keep pace with evolving domains and emerging concepts. Additionally, the vocabulary may limit the ability to include new or evolving concepts, leading to a misunderstanding or misrepresentation.

5.3.3 Taxonomies

In an IA practice, controlled vocabularies and metadata standards are often structured hierarchically as a taxonomy for information organization and retrieval. The National Information Standards Organization (2010) defines a taxonomy as "A collection of controlled vocabulary terms organized into a hierarchical structure. Each term in a taxonomy is in one or more parent/child (broader/narrower) relationships to other terms in the taxonomy" (p. 5). Taxonomies are generally organized hierarchically or poly-hierarchically. Controlled vocabulary terms are organized within the taxonomy, typically in a tree-like structure with broader categories at the top and increasingly specific categories branching out below. Each term in the controlled vocabulary represents a node in the taxonomy hierarchy. The hierarchy can be mixed—not necessarily strictly broader/narrower relationships; cross-references can be defined and terms for a website taxonomy can be added or deleted more easily than in a controlled vocabulary like we might find in a library system.

5.3.4 Faceted Classification

Faceted Classification is used by many IAs who are organizing websites or search tools (Hearst, 2009; Tunkelang, 2009). We see these quite often in online ecommerce and library systems. In faceted classification, we provide additional terms to help the user efficiently find what they want. Think about your online shopping experiences. Do you search for shoes and then scroll through every result? Probably not, even in a hierarchy you may find hundreds or thousands of items at each level (e.g., Shoes > Hiking shoes). More likely you narrow down your searches using facets, like size or color.

By definition, faceted classification classifies information objects by concepts from multiple orthogonal categories (called facets). Orthogonal means *mutually exclusive* and is

Fig. 5.5 Facets on the left side of the screen (Brands and size) help the user find their desired results

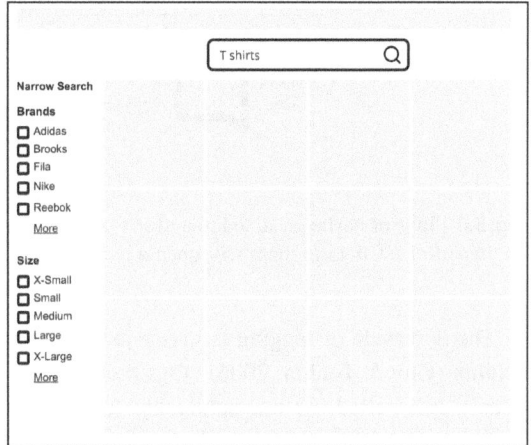

fundamental to faceted classification. This means facets cannot overlap. Ideally, each facet should also be a complete description of the area it covers. An information object can be described by one and only one category within each facet (for example, a particular item in e-commerce cannot be both a shirt and pants). But in practice, both orthogonality and completeness might be difficult to achieve. Many e-commerce sites (Fig. 5.5), libraries, and other organizations adopted faceted classification to provide additional "access points" to their holdings, meaning labels or terms that can be used to find objects.

5.3.5 Tagging

Tagging (Trant, 2009), and social curation (Zarro & Hall, 2012), has become an integral part of the user experience in many information systems, particularly in social media. Contrasted to professionally developed taxonomies and controlled vocabularies, tagging results in unstructured categories that are free of "control." Users can use whatever terms they like to label web pages, images, social media posts and so on. Uniformity and organizing power emerge from the collective categorizing activities of the user community (Fig. 5.6).

Collections of tags are called "folksonomies," a term coined by Thomas Vander Wal and can be particularly useful in emergent or popular culture topics where terms may not be a part of previously developed vocabularies or taxonomies. Organizations like the Library of Congress and Smithsonian have even used tagging and social media posts to provide new crowd sourced terms and descriptions for previously unidentified assets in their collections (Kalfatovic, et al., 2009; Springer et al., 2008).

Fig. 5.6 Tags or hashtags added to a user's post. Notice the terms preceded by the hash symbol (#) are hyperlinks. Clicking them will open a results page that have similar tags

The downside of tagging is messiness, motivation issues, scalability and global applicability (Guy & Tonkin, 2006). Tags created by a user may be very personal (e.g. "read_later"), misspelled, or not applicable to a wide audience (Marlow et al., 2006). Even with these limitations, tagging has become an important part of today's digital landscape. Although a major motivation of tagging is for personal use, according to a study by Golder and Huberman (2006) the pattern of tags emerges rather early and remains stable over time. A valuable side-product of tagging is that the aggregation statistics also reveal a lot of otherwise implicit relationship, such as:

- **Popularity**: How many people have tagged this resource?
- **Interests**: What tags have been applied to this resource?
- **Community**: Who has used what tags for this resource?

User created tags complement indexing by experts and together they can deliver the best of both worlds. Multiple tags provide additional access points which may match other users' concepts of an object, while professional cataloging usually requires fitting the object to one unique location in a hierarchy. Using both together in a folksonomy can produce excellent results.

5.4   Navigation Systems

The purpose of navigation is to help users move around, reach the information they want, and show their context or location. Navigation shows connections in information organization structures. Because users come to a system with different motivations, they need multiple ways to navigate, helping to answer the following questions:

- Where am I? (orientation)
- What can I do? (content, interaction, search)
- Where can I go from here? (go up, move laterally, drill down)

5.4.1 Navigation Types

Navigation can be within one information space, across several information spaces, or the entire digital landscape. For information architects, navigation design often focuses on within-site/app navigation (Fig. 5.7).

Global navigation brings together the key set of access points that users might need to get from one end of the site to the other. Anywhere you want to go, you can get there (eventually) from the global navigation (When users get lost, they often go back to the global navigation and start over again).

Local navigation includes page-level navigation and contextual navigation. *Page-level navigation* helps the user easily move around different sections of the page. On descriptive pages there could be an overview/anchor links on the top or on the side, back to top links, etc. For pages with large datasets (e.g., a search results page) UI elements should be available for comparing, sorting, and selecting.

Contextual navigation follows content and context, rather than structures. The links are usually embedded in the context of the content (via inline links) or displayed in a specific area of the page (e.g., associative links for related items), commonly seen on the right-hand side, on the upper right corner, or at the bottom of the page. This type of navigation supports associative learning.

Supplemental navigation includes sitemaps, site indexes, FAQs, tutorials, or in-page links. Sitemaps and site indexes were more commonly seen in early websites. Sitemaps are generally considered a top-down approach to content organization while site indexing is a bottom-up approach. Thus, sitemaps emphasize overview functions where site indexing will provide more details (Fox, 2003).

Process navigation that guides the user through a serial, multi-step process to complete a complex task is called process navigation. A process step indicator (navigation bar) is often used to provide an overview to users about where they are and what they need to go through to finish the process.

Fig. 5.7 Website navigation types and typical locations

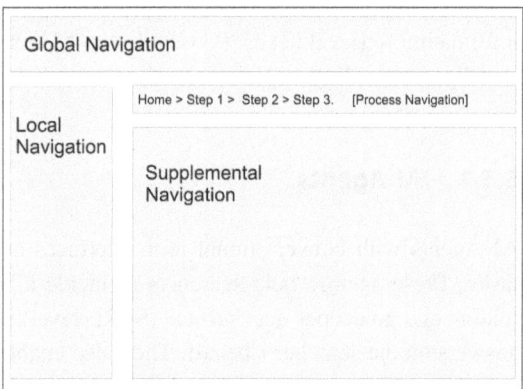

5.5   Search Systems

Searching is a means for the user to access content, web pages, or files using keyword queries. With a search engine, users can bring related results together instantly by entering keywords and then browsing through the results. However, having a good search engine alone does not guarantee that the user will be successful. There are many factors that impact the user's searching behavior.

- Users do not always know what information they need. In other words, they do not know what they are searching for.
- Users need to express their needs in queries. Queries stated in a few words are not the best way to represent one's information needs (Belkin et al., 1982).
- Search engines need to index content appropriately, but there is no one optimized indexing method that will work best for all users' queries.
- Search results need to be displayed in a way that users understand.

As an information architect, one big challenge is to communicate to content owners and users what search engines can and cannot do. Additionally, users may interact with search in unexpected ways. Broder (2002) defined three categories of web search: navigational, informational, and transactional, which IAs should account for in search and navigation design.

- **Navigational**: A "known item" search, where the goal is to reach a specific site or content known to be available.
- **Informational**: A search meant to retrieve and learn new information. This is probably the type of search we think of when considering search systems.
- **Transactional**: A search meant to further shopping, downloading and similar activities.

In short, search cannot solve wayfinding problems in websites, apps, enterprise software—or any information space. Search and navigation should work together to support information retrieval needs. Powerful new AI technologies are now included in the search paradigm, providing opportunities for IAs to help deliver even more useful search tools.

5.5.1   AI Agents

AI Agents with conversational user interfaces are used to help people complete search tasks. These agents "help searchers to tackle a broader range of tasks than information finding and go deeper than surface (SERP-level) interactions with content by synthesizing answers on the searcher's behalf. They also enable searchers to communicate their intents and goals more directly" (White, 2024, AI Agents section). Agents can take on the guise of a chatbot or look more like a traditional search box.

Unlike a search engine that produces a list of links, the conversational nature of AI agents synthesizes information from many resources, retains context, and supports following up in a sequence of queries (Spatharioti, et al., 2023). Whereas before users would search and get a list of links and click through in an exploratory or berrypicking (Bates, 1989) fashion, AI agents give users a comprehensive answer in a single interface. While this is undoubtedly a leap forward in search, we must ensure that they provide correct answers and support in critical areas like healthcare (Rahsepar et al., 2023).

Examples of benefits AI agents provide include:

- **Guided Search**: Agents can refine search queries and provide more relevant results. For example, a travel chatbot might ask about locations and travel dates to offer personalized travel recommendations.
- **Natural Language**: Agents utilize natural language processing (NLP) techniques to understand and interpret user queries expressed in natural language, supporting complex queries.
- **Information Retrieval**: Agents can retrieve and synthesize information from many sources in response to user queries. Leveraging user behavior and preferences, they can provide personalized results.
- **Contextual Navigation**: Agents can streamline navigation by providing guidance or shortcuts to pages, features, or resources within an application or website.
- **Assistance**: Agents can assist users completing tasks by offering step-by-step instructions and may even escalate to human customer support when a serious issue is detected. For example, a banking chatbot may fetch a human representative for fraud related queries (Fig. 5.8).

Overall, AI Agents can transform search and navigation experiences by providing personalized assistance, understanding natural language, synthesizing content, and offering personalized results and guidance.

5.6   Summary

Organizing information spaces is a fundamental part of Information Architecture. Luckily, IAs can draw from the library sciences and other areas for understanding and best practices, like using logical organization structures and metadata standards. Controlled vocabularies, taxonomies, and faceted search are used by IAs to provide top-down structure, while tagging and social classification give users powerful ways to add bottom-up

Fig. 5.8 An AI agent providing assistance for potential fraud

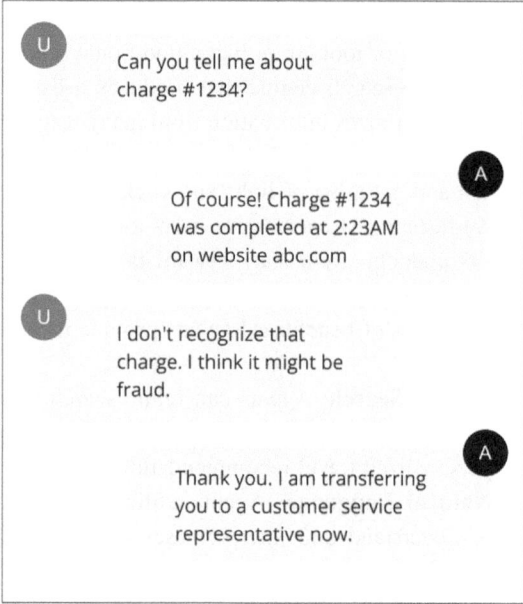

organization. Navigation and search help users traverse through spaces to find information, while AI agents offer exciting opportunities to enhance the user experience and provide accelerated pathways to finding and learning.

References

Bates, M. J. (1989). The design of browsing and berrypicking techniques for the online search interface. *Online Information Review, 13*(5), 407–424. https://doi.org/10.1108/eb024320

Belkin, N. J., Oddy, R. N., & Brooks, H. M. (1982). ASK for information retrieval: Part I. Background and theory. *Journal of Documentation, 38*(2), 61–71.

Broder, A. (2002). A taxonomy of web search. *In SIGIR Forum, 26*(2), 3–10.

ExLibris. (2024). *Artificial intelligence blog series: Introducing our AI generated metadata.* https://exlibrisgroup.com/blog/artificial-intelligence-blog-series-introducing-our-ai-metadata-generator/.

Fox, C. (2003). *Sitemaps and site indexes: What they are and why you should have them.* Boxes and Arrows. http://boxesandarrows.com/sitemaps-and-site-indexes-what-they-are-and-why-you-should-have-them/.

Gilliland-Swetland, A., Bacca, M., & Gill, T. (2000). *Introduction to metadata: Pathways to digital information.* Getty Information Institute.

Golder, S. A., & Huberman, B. A. (2006). Usage patterns of collaborative tagging systems. *Journal of Information Science, 32*(2), 198–208. https://doi.org/10.1177/0165551506062337

Guy, M., & Tonkin, E. (2006). Folksonomies: Tidying up tags? *D-Lib Magazine, 12*(1). Retrieved from http://www.dlib.org/dlib/january06/guy/01guy.html.

Hearst, M. A. (2009). *Search user interfaces.* Cambridge University Press.

International Organization for Standardization. (2017). *Information and documentation—The Dublin core metadata element set.* Part 1: Core elements. (ISO Standard No. 15836-1:2017). https://www.iso.org/standard/71339.html.

Kalfatovic, M. R., Kapsalis, E., Spiess, K. P., Van Camp, A., & Edson, M. (2009). Smithsonian team Flickr: A library, archives, and museums collaboration in web 2.0 space. *Archival Science, 8*(4), 267–277.

Kipfer, B. A. (1997). *The order of things: How everything in the world is organized... Into hierarchies, structures, & pecking orders.* Random House.

Marlow, C., Naaman, M., Boyd, D., & Davis, M. (2006). HT06, tagging paper, taxonomy, Flickr, academic article, to read. In *Proceedings of the seventeenth conference on hypertext and hypermedia* (pp. 31–40). http://doi.acm.org/10.1145/1149941.1149949

National Information Standards Organization. (2010). *Guidelines for the construction, format, and management of monolingual controlled vocabularies.* https://groups.niso.org/higherlogic/ws/public/download/12591/z39-19-2005r2010.pdf.

Rahsepar, A. A., Tavakoli, N., Kim, G. H. J., Hassani, C., Abtin, F., & Bedayat, A. (2023). How AI responds to common lung cancer questions: ChatGPT versus google bard. *Radiology, 307*(5), e230922.

Riley, J. (2017). *Understanding metadata: What is metadata, and what is it for?: A primer.* National Information Standards Organization. https://www.niso.org/publications/understanding-metadata-2017.

Spatharioti, S. E., Rothschild, D. M., Goldstein, D. G., & Hofman, J. M. (2023). *Comparing traditional and llm-based search for consumer choice: A randomized experiment.* arXiv preprint arXiv: 2307.03744.

Springer, M., Dulabahn, B., Michel, P., Natanson, B., Reser, D., Woodward, D., & Zinkham, H. (2008). *For the common good: The library of congress Flickr pilot project.* Library of Congress. https://permanent.fdlp.gov/LPS108390/LPS108390/www.loc.gov/rr/print/flickr_report_final.pdf.

Trant, J. (2009). Studying social tagging and folksonomy: A review and framework. *Journal of Digital Information, 10*(1). Retrieved from http://journals.tdl.org/jodi/article/view/269/278.

Tsay, J., Braz, A., Hirzel, M., Shinnar, A., & Mummert, T. (2020). Aimmx: Artificial intelligence model metadata extractor. In Proceedings of the 17th international conference on mining software repositories (pp. 81–92). https://dl.acm.org/doi/10.1145/3379597.3387448

Tunkelang, D. (2009). *Faceted search.* Springer Nature https://doi.org/10.2200/S00190ED1V01Y20 0904ICR005.

White, R. W. (2024). *Advancing the search frontier with AI agents.* arXiv preprint. https://doi.org/10.48550/arXiv.2311.01235.

Wu, J., Williams, K. M., Chen, H. H., Khabsa, M., Caragea, C., Tuarob, S., Ororbia, A. G., Jordan, D., Mitra, P., & Giles, C. L. (2015). Citeseerx: Ai in a digital library search engine. *AI Magazine, 36*(3), 35–48. https://doi.org/10.1609/aimag.v36i3.2601

Wu, M., Brandhorst, H., Marinescu, M. C., Lopez, J. M., Hlava, M., & Busch, J. (2023). Automated metadata annotation: What is and is not possible with machine learning. *Data Intelligence, 5*(1), 122–138. https://doi.org/10.1162/dint_a_00162

Zarro, M., & Hall, C. (2012). Exploring social curation. *D-Lib Magazine, 18*(11/12). https://doi.org/10.1045/november2012-zarro.

Human Information Behavior and Design Implications

Human information behavior (HIB) is, like other disciplines related to Information Architecture (IA) and UX design, its own field of study with a rich history. The study of HIB includes individual's or group's actions and interactions with any information source: other people, books and libraries, mass media, and many others. Just the fact we are sentient beings receiving stimuli from our environment means information behavior is a constant presence in our lives—we are constantly processing and using information (you're doing it right now!).

> Information Behavior is the totality of human behavior in relation to sources and channels of information, including both active and passive information seeking, and information use. Thus, it includes face-to-face communication with others, as well as the passive reception of information as in, for example, watching TV advertisements, without any intention to act on the information given. (Wilson, 2000, p. 49)

Information behavior is independent of information technology, even though behaviors are shaped by the technologies available. While the underlying psychology and biology of information behavior in a human being may remain the same: The *observable behaviors* will change in response to emerging and evolving channels or technology. For example, today we would not study someone's interaction with a network of friends and family by getting a list of all the people they've mailed physical letters—rather we would investigate their email, chat, and social media.

© The Author(s), under exclusive license to Springer Nature Switzerland AG 2025   83
W. Ding et al., *Information Architecture and UX Design*, Synthesis Lectures
on Information Concepts, Retrieval, and Services,
https://doi.org/10.1007/978-3-031-72138-0_6

HIB is more than thinking about designing wireframe screens or user flows for a single application. Considering a wide range of HIB during the creation and design of an information system will guide design decisions and help develop questions for user research. In earlier chapters, we emphasized that there is nothing more important than user research in the Information Architecture (IA) and Human-Centered Design (HCD) process. We also examined various methods for user research and usability evaluation as well as their uses in different scenarios. In this chapter, we discuss how to apply certain empirical findings resulting from foundational research to IA design. There are two types of empirical data IAs can use:

- **Primary Research**: The findings and recommendations based on your own research in a very specific context (for your systems).
- **Secondary Research**: Research findings and guidelines that are widely acknowledged or adopted in the industry or reported in academic papers.

While the former takes precedence in a specific design project our focus here is on the latter, which can be generalized across all of Information architecture (IA) and UX design. Note, these findings and guidelines either come from repeated empirical studies and/or are based on theories and principles from information science, HCI and other related disciplines. Experienced IAs take advantage of both their own primary research and secondary research like we see in this chapter to inform their designs.

6.1 Understanding User Needs and Information Behavior

Why do we need to spend so much time and energy trying to understand users? For two main reasons:

- You are not your users. Be extremely cautious when making assumptions about users. By learning about them through research, IAs make more data-driven decisions.
- Users are diverse—their demographics, goals, attitudes, behaviors, preferences, knowledge, skills, social contexts, and many other characteristics can be distinctive, all of which influence design. Identify and prioritize user types. Create scenarios and flows for each user type and try to learn as much as possible about your users in context.

However, users are also the same in some ways—sharing many traits defined by human emotion, psychology, and cognition. This chapter covers some of the similarities, the information behaviors intrinsic to humans.

6.2   Human Information Behavior Theories and Principles

In this section, we will introduce several theories and principles that have become influential in the HCI and UX domains. You may see some overlaps between theories, and how others may be combined to help form a broader picture of human users. Some are concerned with what is happening within the mind of the user and their limitations, while others look more at behavioral aspects.

6.2.1   Basic Level Categories

The Basic Level Category (BLC) concept was first developed by Rosch (1973) and is further explained by Lakoff (2008). BLCs are the most efficient level of categorization, because they require the least cognitive effort. They are often somewhere in the middle of a hierarchy, between most general and most specific. An example is the term *bird* This sits between animal and "eagle." What do you picture in your mind when you think of a bird? That illustrates the basic level category, meaning it's the *prototype*. These are the categories that have clear examples that first come to mind, and they are levels that children learn first. For IA, we can think about BLC as good labels aligning with the way people naturally think about categories.

6.2.2   Berry Picking Information Behavior Model

Bates' berry-picking model (1989) is well known in the library and information science field and has been used to explain the pattern of exploratory information discovery. According to Bates, interesting information is scattered like berries in the bushes. A search query, therefore, is continually shifting; users may move through a variety of sources; new information may yield new ideas and new directions; the query is not satisfied by a single last retrieved set of results, but rather by a series of selections and bits of information found along the way. A searcher in this model is "moving through many actions towards a general goal of satisfactory completion of research related to an information need."

6.2.3   Bounded Rationality

Herb Simon (1996)., an economics researcher and Nobel laureate, coined the term "bounded rationality" in his influential book, Sciences of the Artificial first published in the 1950's. Bounded rationality is about the constraints people face, both external and internal, when making a decision. The perfect choice is rarely made—usually there is some compromise—people must "satisfice." With unlimited time and unlimited resources, everyone could make better decisions—but that is not reality, there are always limitations. So, a person makes a decision that is "rational" within the "boundaries" of their situation. Examples of limits/bounds in IA include:

- The information people have available to them
- Cognitive abilities
- Limited time to make a decision

Part of the IAs job is to recognize the ability and limitations of the users in context. Often concepts like bounded rationality point the way towards questions to ask in user research, and towards requirements in design.

6.2.4   Dual Process Theory

Dual process theory, which was developed from research on trust and persuasion in the social psychology domain, provides further insights into the motivations and actions of a user (Chaiken, 1980; Petty & Cacioppo, 1986). Humans store rules, called heuristics (but not the same as Nielsen's 10 heuristics), in their memory that are then used to evaluate information and information sources in whole or in part. Information processing exists on a continuum of heuristics and systematic processing, depending on the information need and bounded by limitations like time or motivation.

An example heuristic for IA is "the first result in a search results page is the best." People have learned over time that the first result is usually good enough, and so they encode that as a rule.

Humans also engage in "systematic processing," which is careful reading and analysis of an information resource. When searching for critically important material like health information for example, people are more likely to go deeper into the material.

6.2.5   Exploratory Search

Exploratory search (Marchionini, 2006; White & Roth, 2009) shows how searching can take place over an extended period of time. The searcher learns as they go, and this learning influences subsequent search sessions. It is sometimes described as searching and browsing combined, because we are looking at search(es) not as a tool but as the satisfaction of need. The user does not know the resources or information resources needed to satisfy the need when they begin a search session. In fact, the searcher may not even know the true information need until they have learned from the resources encountered in searching and browsing.

6.2.6 Fitts' Law

Fitts' Law (1954) states that the time required to move from a starting point to a final target area is a function of the distance to the target and the size of the target. Larger targets and closer targets are faster to select. Therefore, to optimize efficiency, it is better to put targets closer to where they are likely to be used (e.g., put buttons next to the activities they relate to), and to make them larger. While this may seem like common sense, we often see this law violated in design.

6.2.7 Hick's Law

Hick's law, also called the Hick-Hyman law (Hick, 1952; Hyman, 1953), describes the amount of time it takes for a human to make a decision, as a function of all of the choices present: The time it takes to make a decision increases as more alternatives are available. Hick's law is mainly useful for simple decision making, as complexity increases the applicability of the law decreases (Lidwell et al., 2010). The law can be useful when designing for simple, time-sensitive decisions; limit the number of choices.

6.2.8 Information Scent Theory

Information Foraging/Scent Theory, proposed by Card et al. at Xerox PARC (2001), has been widely adopted for design (and it is similar to the berry-picking model). Card uses the analogy of wild animals gathering food to analyze how humans collect information. Like wild animals making optimal decisions on where, when, and how to eat, "informa-vores" (information seekers) constantly make decisions on what kind of information to look for: Whether to stay at the current location, when to move on, which link to follow, and when to finally stop. The decision is made such that the user gets maximum benefit for minimum effort (like the least effort principle). When presented with a list of options users will choose the one that gives them the clearest indication (or strongest scent) that it will take them closer to the information they require.

Information scent is used to predict a path's success. In other words, it is used to describe how people evaluate options when they are looking for information on a website. When presented with a list of options users will choose the one that gives them the clearest indication (or strongest scent) that it will take them closer to the information they require. People will keep clicking as long as they sense that they are getting warmer—the scent must keep getting stronger and stronger or they will give up.

6.2.9 Miller's Magic Number Seven

Miller's (1956) "magic number seven, plus or minus two" demonstrates some of the limitations humans have in terms of memory. The central argument for our purposes is that the average human can only hold seven, plus or minus two, chunks of information in short term memory. This helps explain why phone numbers were broken up into the pattern 555–555–5555, as this could be seen as three chunks, not 10. The point here is not to always limit web pages or menus to seven items, but rather to consider this law when expecting people to recall information, and to know that humans have limits.

However, we do not want to blindly follow this concept in IA. How does 7 ± 2 relate to something like menus on a website? Human beings can only remember a limited amount of information; we are much better at recognition. Might that be why something like large dropdown menus (mega menus), which may seem like they violate 7 ± 2, are effective? Users recognize labels, they do not recall them from memory.

6.2.10 Paradox of Choice: Less Is More

Schwartz (2004) identifies two types of people based on their decision-making patterns:

- Maximizers: Trying to make the best possible decision.
- Satisficers: Selecting the first one meeting minimal requirements. (Note that Simon also used the term satisficing in his exploration of bounded rationality).

While satisficers are content to select products or services that meet a minimum set of requirements, maximizers compare all possible options. According to Schwartz, when there is no choice life is miserable; but with too many choices, other issues come up:

- **Analysis Paralysis**: When there are so many choices, you end up not being able to make a choice quickly. A grocery store did an experiment with two treatments. One was to allow customers to sample 24 or 6 different flavors of jam. With 24 options, more people came to the table but 1/10th as many people actually bought jam than the other setting.
- **Decision Quality**: With too many choices, the decision making process gets exponentially more complex. People tend to adopt the most simple and avoid the complex criteria, but simple ones aren't necessarily the most important criteria. As a result, they end up making a worse decision.
- **Decision Satisfaction**: Doing better and feeling worse. If you managed to overcome paralysis and ensure decision quality, satisfaction is the 3rd factor. When there are more choices, it becomes easier to regret—satisfaction is reduced. If you did not examine ALL options, you assume one or more other options might have been better.

- **Opportunity Cost**: Even though you made the right decision, there is no easy way to tell this is truly better than your next best alternative. That will make you feel less satisfied with your choice.
- **Escalation of Expectations**: Seeing more choices raises expectations. When your expectation is higher than the selection, you experience regret. Schwartz gave an example: In a study on college seniors looking for jobs, maximizers got jobs with $7500 more or 25% higher for their salary, but they felt worse (and were also more pessimistic, overwhelmed, stressed, and disappointed) than the satisficers.

6.2.11 How to Cope with Too Many Choices?

From the designer's perspective, here are the things you can do to help the user:

- Create default settings aligned with users' best interests, because people tend to do nothing when facing multiple choices.
- Use invisible filters (e.g., based on previous behavior, profile preferences) and visible filters (allowing the user to articulate their selection criteria) to limit choices for the user.
- Organize choices hierarchically—because hierarchical structure feels smaller than flat lists so the number of choices is perceived as fewer.

6.2.12 Time Scales

A ten second response system… may be no better for the human than—in some tasks at least—than a one-minute response or a five-minute response. (Miller, 1968, p. 268)

Interaction times have a large influence on people's use and perception of a system. Think about the frustration you feel when experiencing even a few seconds delay submitting an online form, or lengthy buffering in streaming media. Have you ever abandoned an interaction because it just took too long?

Conversely, how about the delight you feel when a mobile app loads instantly and it feels like you're directly controlling the system? Or, the feeling when you get an immediate success message after pressing "submit form." These reactions are sometimes beyond our rational understanding, yet strongly effect our interaction and satisfaction—and thus usability.

6.2.13 Powers of 10

Researchers investigating information systems identified a hierarchy of time scales that influence our interactions, from biological responses to social interactions. Newell and Card (1985) classified human information activities in *"powers of 10"* (p. 226), ranging from the "neural and biochemical" taking place in milliseconds, to the "social and organizational" that take place over weeks to decades. The bands where human–computer interaction mostly falls is between these two; the "psychological," taking place from tenths of second to 10s, and "bounded rationality" (borrowing the term from Herb Simon) taking place from minutes to days. Their colleague, Pirolli (2009, p. 35), summarized this scale for information-seeking systems with approximate times:

- **Social**: Days—months and beyond, e.g., social systems involving many factors including coordination, trust, and reputation
- **Rational**: Minutes—hours, e.g., task structures and longer-term goals
- **Psychological**: 100 ms–10 s, e.g., perception and cognition
- **Biological**: 1–99 ms, e.g., neurons firing in the human brain

Similarly, Nielsen (2009) gives clear examples of how we can use the powers of 10 in UX design, including:

- **Milliseconds:** "To create the illusion of direct manipulation, a user interface must be faster than 0.1 s."
- **Seconds:** "During 1-s response times, users retain the feeling of being in control of the interaction even though they notice that it's a 2-way interaction."
- **10 Seconds**: "After 1 s, users get impatient and notice that they're waiting for a slow computer to respond. The longer the wait, the more this impatience grows; after about 10 s, the average attention span is maxed out."

This interaction hierarchy helps us understand how systems influence people over time, from the psychological and rational which has long been the center of IA and UX designers, to the longer social band with is the focus of *systems thinkers* (Chap. 8). Additionally, clear guidelines give us specific requirements we can give to engineers and developers—much better than saying *make it fast*.

The Doherty threshold, that *productivity soars when response times are less than 400* ms, based on research at IBM, has been adopted by many in our field as a simple way to communicate the need for speed (Doherty & Thadhani, 1982). Drilling down to perceptions in the biological range, Lindgaard et al. (2006) found people can start making decisions about a web page visual design in *50* ms. More recently, Google's User-centric performance metrics (Walton, 2019) provide "defining metrics" that follow the research above, providing objective measures for "fast" or "speed" that can be readily adopted by engineering and design teams, and have been attributed to improved business outcomes.

Taking all of the guidelines and powers of 10, UX designers have strong metrics to use as requirements and share with stakeholders to use when measure time and its impact on user experience.

6.2.14 Zipf's Law, the Principle of Least Effort

Zipf's Law is also thought of as the principle of least effort in IA. In Zipf's words (1949), "Every individual when considering a course of action, will choose the action that requires the least amount of effort." This principle has been widely cited in the library and information science literature to explain user information seeking behaviors. There are two well-known conclusions based on this principle: One is the 80/20 rule: Among all the information sources available, people use 20% of them for 80% of their information needs. The other conclusion is people will choose easily available information sources of relatively low quality over expending the effort necessary to access higher quality sources.

Rather than complaining that people are lazy, we should acknowledge that users are efficiency driven. From a design perspective, it could also help us prioritize user tasks and goals. At the same time, we need to understand this is a strategy for survival but not for excellence. It may not apply to all situations.

6.2.15 Theories Summary

The theories above represent some of the ways academics distilled empirical data into characterizations of HIB information spaces; representing within the mind, social or psychological, and behavioral concepts. All have a relation, of varying degrees, information system design. In addition to the academic theories above, interaction design has its own set of guidelines and principles, which we will discuss in following chapters.

6.3   Design Implications

Our knowledge about human information behavior informs the design to better meet the user needs and minimize user frustration. Here, are some general design guidelines:

- Create structure and navigation to meet users' mental model and expectations.
- Design to support quick scanning and strong information scent.
- Help people learn what they don't know.
- Set up the right default settings.

- Ensure the system response times are in acceptable limits for the task at hand.
- Allow people time for decision-making and motivate people to complete transactions. For example, by narrowing down options and supporting easy comparison between objects, saving unfinished shopping carts for users between sessions in e-commerce environments, or showing actual number of items remaining in lists, like search results or in large easily browsed collections.

6.3.1 Web Use Considerations

Because the web is such an important part of the information landscape, we share considerations for web design and search below. Long before the invention of the web, information scientists and HCI researchers started studying user information behavior. The growth of the web, however, made the user population "explode" quickly and created additional usage patterns as well. The following patterns are summarized based on the studies at different times in various contexts. Note most of these findings were more focused on non-repeated uses of public websites. Some of them may not be completely applicable to frequent and expert users of a website.

6.3.2 Web Users Don't Read Pages. They Scan

Much of web use is motivated by the desire to quickly find information. Users just don't have the time or patience to read any more than necessary. Nielsen's (2006) eye tracking study with 200+ web users identified a strong "F" shaped reading pattern. Users first read in a horizontal movement, usually across the upper part of the content area. This initial element forms the F's top bar. Next, users move down the page a bit and then read across in a second horizontal movement that typically covers a shorter area than the previous movement. This additional element forms the F's lower bar. Finally, users scan the content's left side in a vertical movement (Fig. 6.1).

6.3.3 Web Users Don't Make Optimal Choices. They Satisfice

Satisficing is seeking information that is good enough. Unlike the general rational decision-making model, which includes identifying a problem, gathering information, identifying the possible solutions, and choosing the best one (sometimes called "optimizing" or "maximizing") web users are often in a hurry and tend to adopt a satisficing model. In addition, there's usually not much of a penalty for guessing wrong in the web environment. However, satisficing behavior is even used by people like firefighters, pilots,

Fig. 6.1 The "F" shaped reading pattern, observed with eye-tracking tools in one of the author's studies

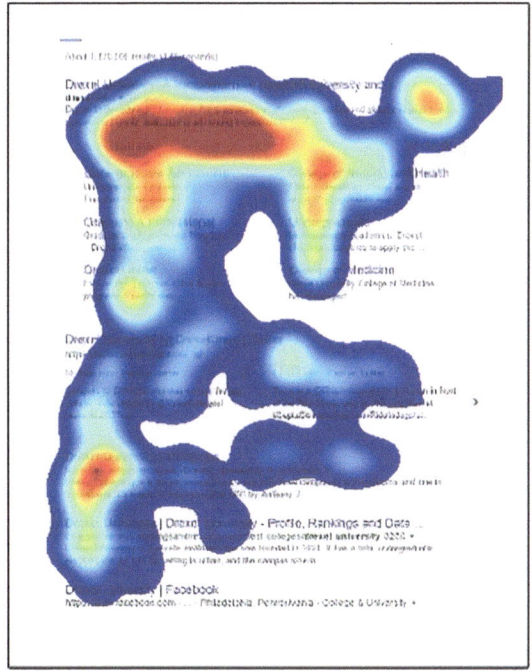

chess masters, and nuclear power plant operators (Krug, 2005). These people make high-stakes decisions in real settings with time pressure, vague goals, limited information, and changing conditions. They do not compare options. Instead, they take the first reasonable plan that comes to mind and do a quick mental test for problems.

6.3.4 How Do People Search the Web?

Web search is no longer just "10 blue links." (Oliveira & Lopes, 2023a). Rather, search results pages have evolved heavily over the past 20 years, becoming a more sophisticated and complex, while providing answers directly on the page (Oliveira & Lopes, 2023b). AI agents meanwhile, offer new experiences for searchers by synthesizing and delivering personalized results in a conversational interface (White, 2024).

Web search engines now provide content like images, news snippets, and map data directly on the results page, in addition to links out to the resulting webpages. These features have substantially changed how people interact with search over the years. Table 6.1 shows a recent summary of findings about how people search on Google, which accounts for a large majority of the global search market (Semrush, 2024).

Table 6.1 Results from a study of Google search by Semrush (2024)

	Desktop	Mobile
Search words per query	1–2 (31.6%); 3–4 (38.2%); 5–6 (17.1%)	1–2 (31%) 3–4 (39.9%) 5–6 (18%)
Time to make a decision	45% take between 0 and 5 s 20% between 5 to 10 s	33% take between 0 and 5 s 18% between 5 to 10 s
Reformulation: initial searches are refined	17.9% of queries	29.3% of queries
"Zero clicks," where it's assumed the user found an answer on the search results page without clicking through	25.6% of searches	17.3% of queries

6.3.5 Design for Search Systems

Users browse by following links and search to find information in traditional search engines. For our purposes, search is one of many IA components that work together to make the website/application achieve much higher performance than the sum of the individual systems. When designing a search interface, the following issues need to be considered:

- **How long should the search box be?** Do long queries lead to better search results? Longer search boxes invite more search terms, however, long natural language searches may not be better. When the number of search terms reaches a certain threshold, the number of search results can drop dramatically, and it does not guarantee most relevant results.
- **How many search boxes are needed?** Sometimes multiple search boxes can appear in an interface. Figure 6.2 shows people search and site search boxes on a University's intranet. Which one is better, one search box or multiple? One search box is almost always better. With faceted search and sorting, multiple search boxes can be combined.
- **Should we provide search assistance/shortcuts?** Search assistance, such as auto-complete/typeahead, spell checking, stemming, search histories, and thesaurus searching can be very helpful to the user. The common "did you mean" feature which corrects spelling is a good example of assistance.
- **Should we design for advanced search?**
- Given that only a small number of people use advanced search features, keyword search should be the default. Advanced search may be made available via a link or other control, but do not count on people using it.
- **How to display meaningful search results?**
- When the search is against multiple sources, the search results can be displayed corresponding to the source/type, such as showing images, news, and video. Faceted search

Fig. 6.2 An Intranet site with two search boxes. Can we be sure users know which to search?

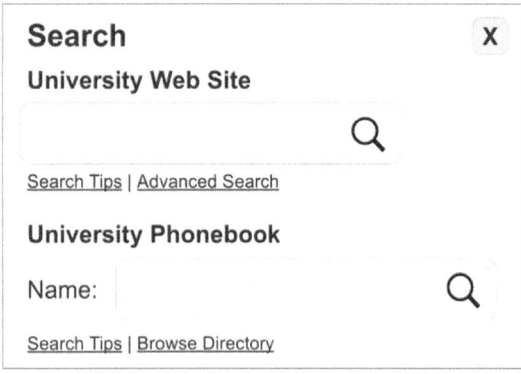

with filters and sorting helps users drill down to meaningful results. Sorting also supports exploration of search results. Additionally, showing the query term highlighted in results summaries can be helpful.

6.4 AI for Search

Search is an area that will be fundamentally changed by Generative AI (GenAI). However substantial "practical, technical, and legal challenges" remain to be solved before GenAI can match the scale of a search engine like Google (Gurdeniz & Hosanagar, 2023). For example, retraining models on new data is expensive and time consuming; the data used must be curated to be timely, factually correct, and unbiased; and copyright law may limit the ability to train models without licensing agreements. While it seems that web search is likely to remain a big part of how people access information for years to come, anticipating future changes Google (2024) analyzed its data after launching the Generative AI tool Gemini, and reported four trends:

- "The "exactly-what-I-want" search:" Searches with five or more words grew 1.5 times year over year, as people learn to add more context for the AI engine.
- "Complex search made easy:" Generative AI combines multiple sources into one result, limiting the need to search multiple times—it does the exploratory search for you.
- "Search beyond words:" Visual search by uploading an image, or "circle to search" feature on Android devices.
- "Search beyond answers:" Searches for people who want contextual guidance not just an answer, for example "rainy day activities."

These trends suggest that while traditional search results with a list of links is still a big part of people's experience, AI is augmenting that experience and users are adapting to get the benefits of these exciting new technologies. Chatbot/conversational interfaces like those found in ChatGPT, Google Gemini, and Microsoft Co-Pilot are providing a way to solve the age old search conundrum, *people don't want to search, they want answers.*

6.5   Summary

Information behavior theories can be very helpful in providing guidance and background for design. Research from several academic disciplines including psychology, information and library science and economics has provided insights into the human behaviors we see in information spaces that can inform design decisions. As AI technologies like GenAI improves, we can expect it to substantially change how people search and use information on the web.

References

Bates, M. J. (1989). The design of browsing and berrypicking techniques for the online search interface. *Online Information Review, 13*(5), 407–424. https://doi.org/10.1108/eb024320

Card, S. K., Pirolli, P., Van Der Wege, M., Morrison, J. B., Reeder, R. W., Schraedley, P. K., & Boshart, J. (2001). Information scent as a driver of Web behavior graphs: results of a protocol analysis method for Web usability. In *Proceedings of the SIGCHI conference on human factors in computing systems* (pp. 498–505). ACM.

Chaiken, S. (1980). Heuristic versus systematic information processing and the use of source versus message cues in persuasion. *Journal of Personality and Social Psychology, 39*(5), 752.

Doherty, W. J., & Thadhani, A. J. (1982). *The economic value of rapid response time.* IBM Report.

Fitts, P. M. (1954). The information capacity of the human motor system in controlling the amplitude of movement. *Journal of Experimental Psychology, 47*(6), 381–391. https://doi.org/10.1037/h0055392

Google. (2024). *Search in the Gemini era: 4 trends powered by generative AI.* https://www.thinkwithgoogle.com/marketing-strategies/search/generative-ai-search-trends-and-transformations/.

Gurdeniz, E., & Hosanagar, K. (2023). Generative AI won't revolutionize search—Yet. *Harvard Business Review.* https://hbr.org/2023/02/generative-ai-wont-revolutionize-search-yet.

Hick, W. E. (1952). On the rate of gain of information. *Quarterly Journal of Experimental Psychology, 4*(1), 11–26.

Hyman, R. (1953). Stimulus information as a determinant of reaction time. *Journal of Experimental Psychology, 45*(3), 188.

Krug, S. (2005). *Don't make me think: A common sense approach to web usability* (2nd ed.). New Riders Press.

Lakoff, G. (2008). *Women, fire, and dangerous things: What categories reveal about the mind.* University of Chicago Press. Retrieved from http://books.google.com/books?id=TomacQAACAAJ.

Lidwell, W., Holden, K., & Butler, J. (2010). *Universal principles of design.* Rockport Publishers.

Lindgaard, G., Fernandes, G., Dudek, C., & Brown, J. (2006). Attention web designers: You have 50 milliseconds to make a good first impression! *Behaviour and Information Technology, 25*(2), 115–126.

Marchionini, G. (2006). Exploratory search: From finding to understanding. *Communications of the ACM, 49*(4), 41–46.

Miller, G. A. (1956). The magical number seven, plus or minus two: Some limits on our capacity for processing information. *Psychological Review, 63*(2), 81. https://web-archive.southampton. ac.uk/cogprints.org/730/1/miller.html.

Miller, R. (1968). Response time in man-computer conversational transactions. In *Proceedings of the December 9–11, 1968, fall joint computer conference, Part I* (AFIPS' 68 (Fall, part I)), (pp. 267–277). https://doi.org/10.1145/1476589.1476628.

Newell, A., & Card, S. K. (1985). The prospects for psychological science in human-computer interaction. *Human-Computer Interaction, 1*(3), 209–242.

Nielsen, J. (2006). *F-shaped pattern for reading web content* (original study). https://www.nngroup. com/articles/f-shaped-pattern-reading-web-content-discovered/.

Nielsen, J. (2009). *Powers of 10: Time scales in user experience.* https://www.nngroup.com/articles/ powers-of-10-time-scales-in-ux/.

Oliveira, B., & Teixeira Lopes, C. (2023a). From 10 blue links pages to feature-full search engine results pages-analysis of the temporal evolution of SERP features. In *Proceedings of the 2023 conference on human information interaction and retrieval* (pp. 338–345). https://doi.org/10.1145/ 3576840.3578307.

Oliveira, B., & Teixeira Lopes, C. (2023b). The evolution of web search user interfaces-an archaeological analysis of google search engine result pages. In *Proceedings of the 2023 conference on human information interaction and retrieval* (pp. 55–68). https://doi.org/10.1145/3576840.357 8320.

Petty, R. E., & Cacioppo, J. T. (1986). The elaboration likelihood model of persuasion. *Advances in Experimental Social Psychology, 19*, 123–205.

Pirolli, P. (2009). Powers of 10: Modeling complex information-seeking systems at multiple scales. *Computer, 42*(3), 33–40.

Rosch, E. H. (1973). Natural categories. *Cognitive Psychology, 4*(3), 328–350.

Schwartz, B. (2004). *The paradox of choice.* HarperCollins.

Semrush. (2024). *34 eye-opening google search statistics for 2024.* https://www.semrush.com/blog/ google-search-statistics/.

Simon, H. (1996). *The sciences of the artificial* (3rd ed.). MIT Press.

Walton, P. (2019). *User-centric performance metrics.* https://web.dev/articles/user-centric-perfor mance-metrics.

White, R. W., & Roth, R. A. (2009). *Exploratory search: Beyond the query-response paradigm.* Springer Nature.

White, R. W. (2024). *Advancing the search frontier with AI agents.* arXiv:2311.01235. https://doi. org/10.48550/arXiv.2311.01235.

Wilson, T. D. (2000). Human information behavior. Informing. *Science, 3*(2), 49–56.

Zipf, G. K. (1949). *Human behavior and the principle of least effort: An introduction to human ecology.* Addison-Wesley.

7

IxD is a broad concept, emphasizing the interaction between people and the interface, and how all the elements come together in the context of use. The Interaction Design Association defines Interaction Design (IxD) as follows:

> It is the design of the interaction between users and products. Most often when people talk about interaction design, the products tend to be software products like apps or websites. The goal of interaction design is to create products that enable the user to achieve their objective(s) in the best way possible. (Teo, 2024)

IxD emerged from under the umbrella of User Experience (UX) Design and User Interface Design (aka "man–machine interaction" or "human–computer interaction"); and is concerned about the *user's control and system response*. Information architecture (IA) on the other hand emphasizes the underlying connections between information elements and related functionalities. However, in our highly connected information societies IA, UX design, and IxD are more and more intertwined together, and the overlap between them is very strong. The Interaction Design we discuss here is mainly focused on the overlapping areas (Fig. 7.1).

7.1 Interaction Design Principles

In order to make sure we get the design right, we turn to interaction design principles, which come at multiple levels. Cooper (2004) categorized them into four levels: *Design values, conceptual principles, behavioral principles and interface level principles.* The

Fig. 7.1 Intersection of UI
design and information
organization

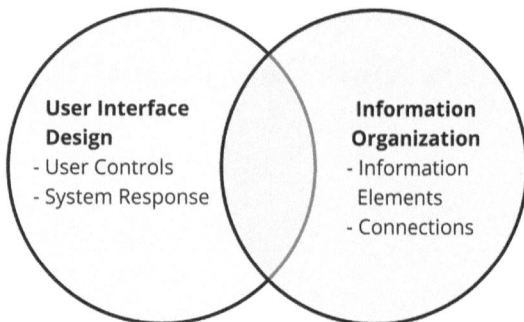

design principles we focus on in this chapter are grounded in the theories we've discussed (Chaps. 5 and 6) and are mainly at behavioral and interface level. Interaction design principles are shared across desktop applications, handhelds, kiosks, TV-based interfaces, automotive interfaces, appliances, audible interfaces and many more. Here we use examples from the web, as web interfaces are a common ground we all share and are applicable to many domains.

7.1.1 Fitts' Law: Design for Fitts'

Fitts' Law (1954) is used to guide the placement of interactive elements. Some guidance it gives when designing an actionable object on the page (e.g., buttons or links):

- **Bigger is better**: Important functions should be presented with large objects/buttons.
- **Closer is faster**: Contextual action buttons or links should be presented within reasonable proximity.
- **Less fine motor control is required**: Correspondingly, when the target is so small or surrounded so closely by other objects, the user will have to slow down the pace to and choose very carefully to avoid errors. Which option in Fig. 7.2 do you think would have the fewest mistakes?

Fig. 7.2 Pagination examples
demonstrating Fitts' law

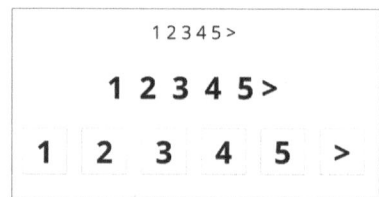

You may think the answer is no brainer, but it really reflects the Fitts' Law—bigger is better. The design with larger clickable areas wins, the larger target makes it easier to acquire. Especially for people with motor disabilities, Fitts' law can help reduce errors by providing larger targets.

7.1.2 Design for Affordance

An affordance points towards whatever action can be taken using an object. Good affordances have "strong visual clues to the operation of things" (Norman, 1998). For example, a chair affords sitting and a button affords pushing. Norman's insight was that perceived affordances are even more important than real affordances in terms of usability. An affordance is only as effective as it is perceivable. In order to ensure perceived affordance the design should meet user expectations, for example by following design patterns.

Affordances can be tricky to design because all users are different. Cultural and other factors influence whether or not the user recognizes an affordance—there is a bit of an art and a science to it. At the same time, make sure non-actionable objects don't have an affordance. Explicit affordance (like text buttons) or implicit affordance (visual cues like icons or context) can be used together to reinforce each other.

Explicit Affordance: Link to Homepage.

Implicit Affordance:

What are good ways to communicate affordances? Shape, color, and font are all ways we do that in information spaces. Location (words and icons in the header of an app often are menu links), grouping actionable items together, remember Hick's Law (1952), and using metaphors, like a shopping cart in eCommerce, are also good ways to communicate affordances.

7.1.3 Design for Efficiency

Efficiency allows the user to accomplish the task quickly. Simply put, make it easier and faster for users to complete tasks. Tognazzini (2001) discusses different ways to ensure efficiency, including decreasing data entry and limiting decision making on the user's side. To decrease data entry, the system can auto-fill information for the user based on previous user activities (Fig. 7.3). Suggesting allowable data ranges or using selections can also save users time and prevent errors. To limit decision making by the user, the system should only present applicable choices (instead of presenting everything and then showing errors after the user selects invalid ones).

Fig. 7.3 Typeahead
functionality saves time and
reduces error (misspellings)

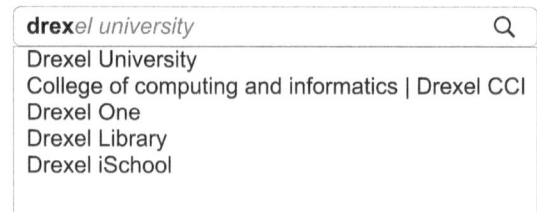

7.1.4   Design for Forgiveness

Forgiveness allows the user to feel less anxiety about making mistakes and allows for imperfections in human activity. Norman (1998) provides a categorization of errors: capture errors, description errors, data-driven errors, associative activation errors, loss-of-activation errors, and mode errors. A perfect match does not exist between humans and computers, so errors will occur and designers must prevent "dead ends" in a system. There are different ways design can help, including the easy reversal of actions, error prevention, and error handling.

7.1.5   Easy Reversal of Actions

Easy reversal of actions protects users from being penalized by mistakes. The system should help users recover, be it an "are you sure" dialog, "undo" or even a "back" button on the web. Designers must balance the reversal of actions with efficiency, evaluating the damage done if the action is not reversible versus the need for efficiency. In Fig. 7.4, most times the user may be okay closing without saving changes—and indeed may want to do that. However, that one time in a hundred—where the student clicks "X" to close without saving the final term paper (or even clicks close by accident)—can have serious consequences. So, designers introduce a little inefficiency to stop a potential catastrophe.

Fig. 7.4 Dialog box prevents a
potential catastrophic error

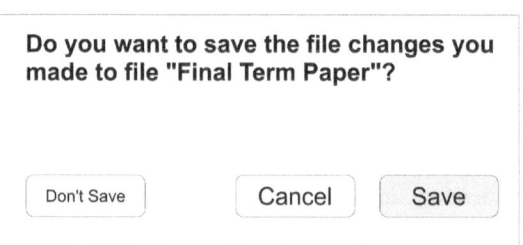

Fig. 7.5 A form with instructions to help prevent errors in the password field

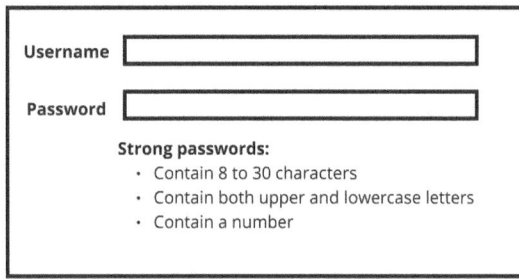

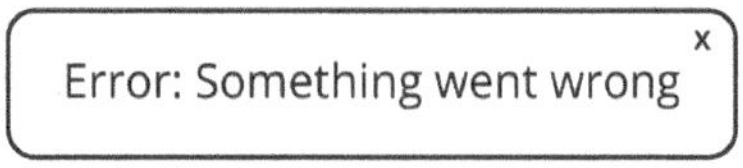

Fig. 7.6 An error message that does not help recovery

Error: Something went wrong ˣ

7.1.6 Error Prevention

Designers should predict common problems and try to prevent them from happening. For example, data entry can be minimized and, therefore, error rate can be minimized when menu selection is offered rather than free form text. Also, it is helpful to instruct the user upfront about certain rules (for example, in password creation, Fig. 7.5). When errors cannot be completely avoided, try to isolate them as much as possible. One of the benefits of step-by-step wizards is to help the user fix the problems that occurred in the current step so that they won't lead to more mistakes in many more subsequent steps for the whole process.

7.1.7 Error Handling

Error handling is the final step in dealing with errors. Error messages should be written to help the user detect the error and offer simple, constructive, and specific instructions for recovery. Do you think Fig. 7.6 is helpful?

7.1.8 Design for User Perceptions

User perceptions are not always right. The things users think/say that happen could be quite different from what actually happens. Secondly, designing engaging experiences for users that spark engagement while reducing anxiety can dramatically increase user satisfaction. User perceptions of time can sometimes be wrong. The story below is cited from Tognazzini (2001):

A classic example occurred in the 1930s in New York City, where "users" in a large new high-rise office building consistently complained about the wait times at the elevators. Engineers consulted concluded that there was no way to either speed up the elevators or to increase the number or capacity of the elevators. A designer was then called in, and he was able to solve the problem.

What the designer understood was that the real problem was not that wait time was too long, but that the wait time was *perceived* as too long. The designer solved the perception problem by placing floor-to-ceiling mirrors all around the elevator lobbies. People now engaged in looking at themselves and in surreptitiously looking at others, through the bounce off multiple mirrors. Their minds were fully occupied and time flew by.

When it comes to time, user perception can be wrong. For example, in one of Tognazzini's studies every user was able to perform a task using the mouse significantly faster than keyboard. However, all of the users reported completing the task much faster using the keyboard. In addition, it is very important to reduce the "subjective" or "perceived" system response time when it cannot really be shortened. He recommends a strategy to keep users engaged and offers tactics for reducing the subjective experience of system "down time." We often see these types of techniques used to show progress status, like a spinning "loading" icon which helps make the wait time less boring and more tolerable.

7.1.9   Design for Help

The best "help" is to make the design intuitive enough so that people do not need help and the UI requires no explanation. Why? We know, based on the least effort principle, only a small number of people will read help documents; we also know people often muddle through difficult systems. Using help slows people down and takes them out of their task flow. They are not interested in learning about the system, they want to complete a task and achieve a goal. However, sometimes help will still be needed. Because people naturally learn best while doing, it is often more useful and effective to provide help in the context of the user task.

7.1.10   Design for Inclusion

Inclusive design means creating information spaces that support people of all ability and background. It requires a strong understanding of different user backgrounds, experiences, and context. It also means designers must reflect on their own abilities and remember that diverse people, very different from them, will use their systems. For example, mobile apps often allow users to change the font size, or a web form may have support for all types of names, like "O'Reilly," that include punctuation. Inclusive design also influences user research, you should aim to get a diversity of feedback to ensure your designs work for all. Microsoft (2016) provides a succinct definition of inclusive design:

Inclusive design: A design methodology that enables and draws on the full range of human diversity.

Most importantly, this means including and learning from people with a range of perspectives.

Designing inclusively doesn't mean you're making one thing for all people. You're designing a diversity of ways for everyone to participate in an experience with a sense of belonging.

Many people are unable to participate in aspects of society, both physical and digital. Understanding why and how people are excluded gives us actionable steps to take towards inclusive design (p. 11).

7.1.11 Design for Personalization and Customization

Personalization and customization are now commonly seen in many online spaces like eCommerce and intranet sites. While the two are closely related and sometimes used interchangeably, we differentiate them for our discussion.

- Personalization is a systematically generated view of the user's own information based on user attributes or activities in the past.
- Customization allows the user to make manual changes, and adjust the look and feel, navigation, and content.

Personalization can be based on the *history of actual user activities* (e.g., past purchase history), or on *voluntary self-reported data* (e.g., demographics, preferences, and interests). While the non-personalized versions contain content for everyone, the personalized version shows a more targeted interface.

Customization allows the user to *choose what to see and when they want to see it*. It is hard to determine how much control is enough for the user—too much control can easily invoke the paradox of choice. Designers need to account for changing user needs, and design good default views given the notoriously low customization rate by the end user.

7.1.12 Interaction Design Components

7.1.12.1 Five Dimensions

Helping to make sense of the components and elements that make up IxD, Crampton-Smith (2007) introduced four dimensions of an interaction design language in Moggridge's book, *Designing Interactions*. Silver (2007) proposed an additional fifth dimension:

Fig. 7.7 Examples of the five dimensions: 1D—The text labels; 2D—Submit button; 3D—The physical mobile device; 4D—Submitting the form, waiting for response; 5D—"Thank you!" response

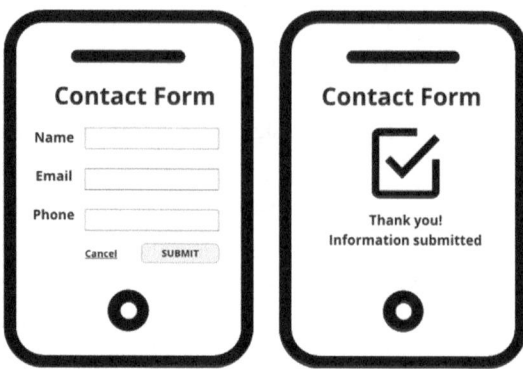

1. **Words**: The text and labels in the interface should be clear, consistent, and have the right "tone of voice," often the work of an Information Architect.
2. **Visual representations**: The graphical elements like images, fonts, buttons and icons should help convey information to users. Visual designers help a lot here.
3. **Physical objects or space**: The devices used for interaction like a laptop screen, keyboard, mouse, or smartphone, and where they are used.
4. **Time**: Motion, sounds, and amount of time spent in an interface.
5. **Behavior**: Bringing together the previous four dimensions, how users interact with the system, and responses to the interaction.

These dimensions are illustrated in simple contact form shown on a mobile device (Fig. 7.7).

7.1.13 Views, Forms, and Workflow

Views are pages used for information viewing and navigation. *Forms* are used for data creation, editing and submission. The controls on the page, such as links and buttons allow the user to interact with the system, such as submit or request data. When different views and forms are combined to support a certain user task, they become a *workflow*. There are different types of workflows: Hubs, wizards, and guides (the combination of hubs and wizards). Hubs (Fig. 7.8) are used when there is a primary view page containing a collection of data elements and a series of one-page forms for editing the elements. Hubs are found in a variety of applications, such as calendars and email. Usually, there is no dependency among the (sub) tasks (forms) in the hub structure.

Fig. 7.8 Hub structure

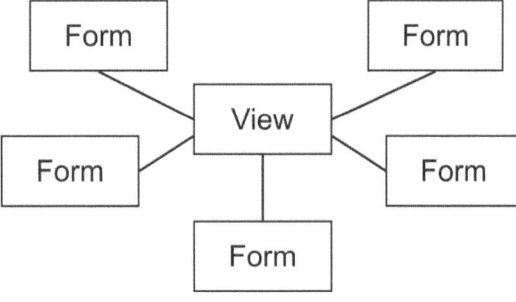

Fig. 7.9 Wizard structure

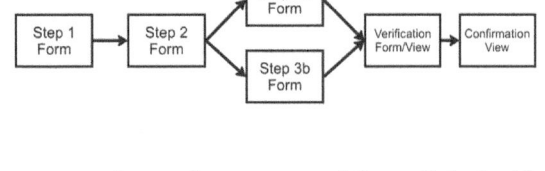

Wizards, also called serial processes, are made up of a sequence of forms linked with "Previous (back)" and "Next (continue)" buttons. Wizards require users to fill out forms one at a time, navigating through the process in a predetermined fixed sequence (shown in Fig. 7.9). After completing all the forms in the sequence, the user is typically taken to a view page summarizing the choices. Typically, the "Shopping cart checking out" process on eCommerce sites takes a wizard approach. It is commonly used for software installation as well. The wizards approach breaks the complex user tasks into multiple simple steps and guides the user through the process.

7.1.14 Filters and Controls

Filters and controls are the devices available on pages for the user to interact with the system. There are many types, including drag and drop, zoom in/out, sliders, buttons, links, checkboxes, expand and collapse, tabs, selection devices, search and filter, auto-complete, and date picker. On the web, sometimes clicking on a control in a webpage navigates to a new page, or sometimes it controls a function that remains on the current page. With dynamic technologies such as Javascript and CSS, web interactions continue to get more and more dynamic and responsive. Users should be made aware of the control's action as much as possible, so they can predict its behavior.

While the interaction design examples we use in this chapter are geared towards the web, they are applicable to almost any interactive systems. An automobile dashboard interface, for example, is likely to follow the hub/wizard structures, and adhere to the interactivity implications presented above. Design patterns, which we discuss next, help designers create new information spaces that remain consistent with interaction design principles, and leverage users' learned behaviors and experiences.

7.2   Design Patterns

The idea of patterns in information sciences largely comes from the influential architect and theorist, Christopher Alexander, who described a "pattern language" for architecture (1979). Patterns provide us the tools and framework for creating beautiful and functional architectures: They are the starting points for design.

Alexander had thousands of years of building and architecture from which to draw his patterns, while IAs have had just a few dozen years. Nevertheless, some patterns are used across many different types of information spaces. You are probably familiar with many of them from using websites and apps, like websites having a footer and header. The benefits of using patterns include (Gerchev, 2012):

- Accelerated process, by reusing components.
- Proven solutions, and increased confidence in the design.
- Encourages consistency.
- Supports communication among team members by using a shared language.
- Novice IAs can utilize proven components.
- Patterns are familiar to users, supporting affordances because the user has experience and learned from them before.

It may be discouraging to think about patterns, on the assumption that designers must always follow that which has come before. Is UX design just copying what already exists? Is it really the case that "consistency is the curse of innovation in design" (Budiu, 2016)? We answer these questions with a resounding *no!*

Remember, information architecture is an art and science. Part of the art is using, reusing, and mashing up patterns and principles into something new. Returning to Alexander's work, think about the thousands of years of history in architecture. If patterns truly are a curse than we would see nothing new, yet every year exciting buildings are constructed that inspire and amaze. Successfully using patterns and principles is more than copying what you've seen in the past; it is creating something new, based on the foundations of what has come before. Think of patterns like the ingredients in a recipe, by combining them in different ways you can get radically different outcomes, even when others have the same ingredients.

Patterns help innovation by providing users a way to transfer skills they've learned in their experiences with other. This helps with adoption—people will more likely try and use a technology where they have some intuitive sense of how it works. Additionally, they will reach proficiency more quickly than if they had to learn the system from the ground up systems (Nielsen, 2000). Apple for example has a long history of creating hardware, software, and apps that *just work,* and they also have a long history of creating detailed design standards for others to follow.

Examining design documentation from Apple and other leading technology companies reveals a truism of IA: *It's very hard to make a design seem effortless.* Balancing the new and old is challenging. Apple's patterns when creating new products like the iPhone were built on established ideas in information architecture, software design, and the web. With some grounding in what had come before, entirely new interactions and devices were born that delighted users.

7.2.1 Responsive Design

Responsive design is a way to serve multiple devices at once, without creating unique websites or apps for each. Rather than design and develop for desktop and tablet, and smartphone, responsive design means we have one codebase (HTML, CSS, JavaScript, etc.) that serves all devices. Some design teams even take a "mobile first" strategy and create for mobile as the primary target, with larger screens secondary, recognizing the sustained importance of mobile devices.

"Breakpoints" define screen resolutions in a responsive design framework, where the layout will change for different sized screens. A good way to find useful breakpoints for a project is to examine web logs for screen resolutions and set breakpoints at the most common sizes for mobile, tablet, desktop, and super-large. UX designers decide at what screen resolution these breakpoints are set and come up with ideas for how the content will display.

Responsive design relies on "grids," which are columns and rows in which elements are placed. As the screen size changes breakpoints are triggered, each "container" in the grid is moved to a location specified by the designer (Fig. 7.10).

Fig. 7.10 Example page grid. As the page resizes, each container in the grid can adapt to the new screen size

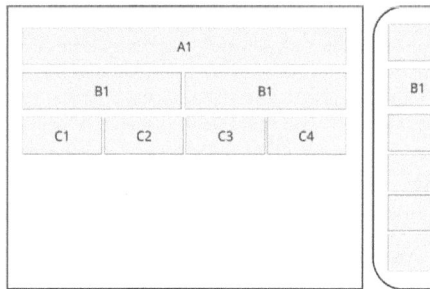

7.2.2   Industry Examples

Leading tech companies provide design systems to help create compelling applications for their devices. This benefits the designer, by delivering validated designs to work with that they know are compatible with the device. The company also benefits because users will have a seamless experience across apps with recognizable elements and controls, regardless of the developer.

- Google has Material design for their devices, https://m3.material.io/
- Apple's guidelines are used for iPads, iPhones and more, https://developer.apple.com/design/human-interface-guidelines/
- Microsoft has a design system for Windows, https://learn.microsoft.com/en-us/windows/apps/design/.

Bootstrap (https://getbootstrap.com/) is a popular HTML, CSS, and JavaScript framework used to develop responsive websites and apps. The framework was originally developed at twitter (now X) and is open-source, meaning anyone can use it for their projects. Thousands of websites today use this framework as a foundation to jumpstart their design and development, because it includes many common elements that most designers and developers need in their designs like buttons, search boxes, and more. For example, Fig. 7.11 was created in minutes using Bootstrap, with interactive elements that should be very familiar.

7.3   Mobile Considerations

Mobile represented a paradigm shift for information technology, and by extension, IA and UX design. The mobile revolution "made any time-anywhere access to information a reality for the vast majority of Americans" (Pew Research Center, 2014). With a mobile

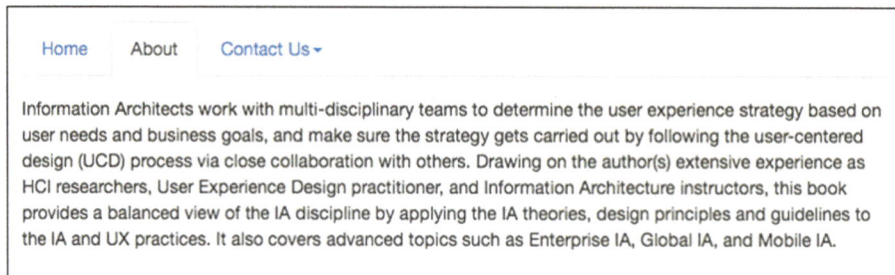

Fig. 7.11 An interactive element created in minutes with Bootstrap

device like a smartphone, and a wireless connection people have an unlimited supply of information at their fingertips anytime and anywhere. Mobile both augments and replaces the desktop computer. Many people live a "mobile first" lifestyle, access via mobile is either their primary or only means of access (Wroblewski, 2012). The convenience of mobile phones makes them the device of choice, even in instances where another more "capable" device is nearby. In this "second screen" scenario, users have a primary device like a TV, and use mobile for social media or other reasons (Gevelber, 2015).

If you are reading this (e)book on a college campus or in a metropolitan area, take a five minute break, but come right back! Walk around for a few minutes and observe the people around you. What did you find? People are everywhere with glowing devices in their hands, texting with friends, playing games, or even doing coursework. Some of them may even be staring at their phones while walking on the sidewalk or even crossing the street. These "distracted walkers" are a sign of how pervasive and addictive mobile devices can be. (American Academy of Orthopaedic Surgeons, 2015).

7.3.1 Smartphone Characteristics

When we reference mobile, we are talking about smartphones. Smartphones are handheld, always on/always connected, with hardware like GPS and cameras, along with the apps to leverage them. They are also personal, often used by a single person. These characteristics give smartphones many advantages, including: GPS helps give location-specific information, they are conveniently almost always at hand and may be used even when a larger computer is likely nearby (Müller et al., 2015; Nylander et al., 2009). Compared to other devices, a smartphone can be inexpensive and easy to start using. Finally, they are adaptable platforms. Developers can leverage stored profiles and hardware to create powerful applications. The user/owner of a smartphone can be uniquely identified, opening the door for many opportunities to employ mobile devices to their full potential, such as mobile ticketing, mobile payment, location based "checkins" and acting as digital keys to, well, open doors. Of course, with the enormous amount of personal information captured on these devices, designers must take care to use the information responsibly and protect user's privacy.

7.3.1.1 Focus on the Mobile Context

IAs should keep mobile's strengths and weaknesses in mind. We've often found ourselves confronted with "desktop" targeted projects and had to advocate for a more balanced desktop/mobile or even mobile-first approach. In these instances reviewing web or usage logs can provide great insights for the correct strategies.

7.3.2 Minimizing the Need for Text Entry

Minimizing user free-form text entry to avoid unnecessary errors has been one of the classical usability best practices all along. However, it becomes critical with the mobile user experience. Mobile users are more likely to make mistakes (due to misspelling or mistyping) or take shortcuts. Mistyping is common, leading to reliance on auto-correct when typing.

Whenever is appropriate, allowing users to input information by making selections instead of entering. Auto-complete or auto-suggest feature is very useful; spelling corrections and abbreviations can help increase error tolerance; whenever possible, the site or the mobile app should provide the following as well: Smart default value based on location (such as zip code), user preferences or history; easy deletion of field values; saving input values from previous sessions or other programs on the mobile phone. Voice input is also increasing in use, replacing typing on the keyboard.

7.3.3 Prioritize Essential Information

Because of the limited screen size and resolution, making best use of the screen real estate becomes critical. Compared to a desktop website, the navigation, widgets and page layout need to be presented more succinctly on the page for ease of use. Similar to the conventional website design, the most frequently used (usually higher level) information should be near the top, where it is most visible and accessible. As the user scans the screen from top to bottom, the information displayed should progress from general to specific and from high level to low level.

7.3.4 Other Mobile Usability Best Practices

- Since the cursor control and positioning mechanism for mobile phones are different, there are additional interesting design challenges. Actionable buttons and controls need to have good spacing between each other. If the controls stay too close together, users must spend extra time and attention being careful where they tap, and they are more likely to tap the wrong element. A simple, easy-to-use user interface should sufficiently space controls and other user-interaction elements so that users can tap accurately with a minimum of effort.
- Maintain consistency between the website, the mobile / responsive design, and native mobile application. That way, users can easily apply what they learned from one channel to another without unnecessary relearning or confusion.

7.3.5   Mobile as the Platform

Given the features and personal nature of smartphones, they have become a platform for a variety of uses beyond information use and seeking. In addition to GPS for location, most smartphones have built-in cameras, and sensors like an accelerometer that measures tilt, motion, and gestures. These sensors can be accessed by mobile apps for a variety of purposes, including games and fitness tracking.

Integration with other devices is another interesting feature of smartphones for IA. An example is as a universal remote control for TV, other multimedia devices and even for controlling room settings (e.g., heating and cooling, lighting). By connecting over WiFi, Bluetooth, or the internet, smartphones can control almost any device near or far given the correct permissions.

7.3.6   User's Wallet

Mobile ticketing enables customers to purchase, order, receive and check tickets anytime and anywhere. It makes the smartphone the ticket, which can be checked or scanned like a paper ticket. Mobile payment, like ApplePay, makes the smartphone function like a user's credit card. By tapping or near field communications, the smartphone initiates payments using options the user has set up in a payment app. Similarly, the smartphone can serve as a customer checkin device. When the user is in a location, they can choose to checkin using an app, creating a notification that they are there.

7.3.7   Mobile and Personalization

Smartphones are naturally suitable for personal information management (PIM) such as address book, emails, messages, and calendar. PIM features have become context and location sensitive. For example, if the user has "buy textbook from bookstore" in a to-do list, when they drive by the bookstore, the smartphone will display a reminder about the book. Another scenario is about a business traveler on a trip. When they pay a restaurant bill with the mobile device, there can be a prompt from the expense management system to ask whether the user wants to capture it for future travel expense reimbursement.

More importantly, the smartphones will continue to get smarter, patiently monitoring your personalized preferences, and delivering information based on a particular situation. For example, the Google maps app can deliver real-time, updated directions to a user driving to a destination, suggesting alternate routes based on updated traffic conditions, road closures, and personal preferences like avoiding tolls.

7.4 Design for AI

With the growing pervasiveness of AI, technology leaders have published several AI design guidelines. Examining the guidelines, you will see many overlaps with human-centered design concepts, demonstrating the universal nature of these principles. In addition, they include concepts like providing ways for users to give feedback on AI output ("Encourage granular feedback"), understanding context ("Remember recent interactions"), and explaining why the AI takes certain actions ("Make clear why the system did what it did"). Examples in parentheses are from the Microsoft guidelines.

- Google "People + AI Research (PAIR):" https://pair.withgoogle.com/guidebook/
- Microsoft "Guidelines for Human-AI Interaction:" https://www.microsoft.com/en-us/haxtoolkit/ai-guidelines/
- Apple: "Machine Learning:" https://developer.apple.com/design/human-interface-guidelines/machine-learning/overview/introduction/
- IBM "Design for AI": https://www.ibm.com/design/ai/

These guidelines have many similarities with each other and with UX design principles, which is not surprising as they are the result of decades of human–computer interaction and AI research. The Microsoft team detailed the process of developing their 18 guidelines: First, synthesizing key concepts from HCI and AI, and then validating them in a study with UX practitioners (Amershi et al., 2019). Weisz and a team at IBM (2024) followed a similar process to produce their six design principles for AI applications. They aim their work at generative AI applications, arguing the previous guidelines do not adequately address use cases in the generative AI space, such as "generative variability" (Weisz et al., 2023)—meaning the outputs of a generative AI application may vary in quality or other characteristics even when the user input does not change.

Big technology companies are driving much of the progress in this space, and the entire field benefits from their work. In an effort to provide "open" guidelines not tied to a corporate entity, Wright and colleagues (2020) compared the work from Google, Microsoft, and Apple. This open initiative gives designers and researchers a forum to collaborate on guidelines while limiting the influence of corporate interests on the outcomes (https://ai-open-guidelines.readthedocs.io/en/latest/). Their results grouped nearly 200 guidelines from the three companies into four main categories for designers to consider:

1. **Initial**: The human values to consider before developing an AI tool, and what users can expect from a system.
2. **Model**: Considerations in the data and model training process, and how this impacts the human user.

3. **Deployment**: How to handle errors, and how to handle user feedback and personalization.
4. **Interface**: Usability and UX design considerations.

While human-centered AI design, like the AI field itself, is evolving rapidly, designers see many benefits from this work. A study of the Google guidelines used by practitioners (Yildrim et al., 2023) suggests two primary benefits. Guidelines are used to establish a *human-centered culture*, including training/learning, supporting cross-functional collaboration in a team, and gaining support, or "buy-in" for design decisions. Designers also use the guidelines to give *specific pointers in product design*, using examples to help solve design challenges. These two areas help give human-centered design a much-needed seat at the AI table, an important step forward for delivering safe, trustworthy, and usable AI tools.

7.5   Research to Design Framework

While primary user research is essential for IA and user experience, IAs can also use the theories, principles, design systems we've covered from Chap. 3 the current chapter. They can use secondary research and their own experience and expertise to collect information and inform design. Here, we present a research to design framework that brings together several concepts we covered, which was first shared at a professional UX workshop (Zarro, 2015). Over the years as researchers and practitioners, we've seen projects where design by committee happens, or design work is not implemented. A common thread in these projects is that when teams understand where the design concepts originate, risks are lowered (but never eliminated) and the chance of success increases.

Our Research to Design framework has three main goals:

- A process for making design decisions.
- A way to reduce uncertainty in decision-making.
- A way to support decisions in team discussions about research and design.

IAs should plan projects to include research and evaluation. Sometimes in practice however, projects rely on a "fingers crossed" approach: The system will be usable even though design decisions are not supported by research. (In this case, witnessing the effects of users interacting with the final product is actually your research and evaluation process—far from ideal.) We may get lucky, *even a broken clock is right twice a day*, but far more likely users will encounter avoidable issues, and the project's success will be less than its potential. Our framework provides a structured approach to making informed design decisions *even when time and resources are limited.*

In our experience primary research is always a clear winner. There is just no substitute for meeting with users and learning from them. However, in many cases other researchers have published relevant research or there is an HCI theory, pattern, or principle available to support design decisions. It's likely that "someone has thought about your problem before and expressed those thoughts somehow" (Bernsen & Dybkjær, 2009), which you can use to augment primary research findings. Combining different methods (called *triangulation*) is very powerful and compelling. Think about the methods below like ingredients in a recipe. You can mix and match them to find what works best.

7.5.1   Five Methods

- **Thinking and Experience**: What do we know as experienced IAs? What do we know we don't know, and how can we find out?
- **Theory**: What can we learn from HCI, IA, and related theories?
- **Patterns and Principles**: What can we reuse from the design patterns and principles we see in similar contexts?
- **Secondary Research**: What can we learn from published academic research with empirical data? What can we learn from published case studies or projects lacking empirical data, outside of our organization? What can we learn from previous projects or research completed within our organization?
- **Primary Research**: What can we learn from our user research and evaluation efforts directly related to the current project? This is the *gold standard*, and we should aim to conduct primary research whenever possible.

Below, we explain the methods in more detail.

7.5.2   Thinking and Experience

Using thinking and experience, an IA can draw upon past experiences to support their design decisions. Bernsen & Dybkjær classify thinking as solving problems, and identifying areas that it may not solve: "Thinking is as much an approach to discovering and solving problems as to deciding that certain problems *cannot* be solved through developer thinking alone but require other sources and methods to be resolved" (2009, p. 123). Designers always use some level of thinking and experience.

I've designed three dozen login forms, I know what this form needs

This is a really complex problem, we'll need extensive research to understand how users will interact with the feature

7.5.3   Theory

Theories offer a way to support decisions using academically supported ideas by sharing the "scientific foundations that underpin good design" (Bowles, 2010). We've listed several important HCI/IA theories and laws in an earlier chapter, and recommend going back to them during a design project to see how they may apply. Over time, it becomes second nature and you may feel like theories are almost collaborators, providing steady guidance. Although our example below may seem extreme it illustrates the powers of theory, imagine designing software to be used in a medical setting or in an airplane cockpit.

> Hick's Law tells me that the more options I have, the longer it takes to make a decision. Let's not put any more links near the 'Abort self-destruction' button.

7.5.4   Patterns and Principles

Across information spaces, UI elements and interaction become standard so it makes sense to follow convention. They are sometimes referred to as "best practices," and remember the saying, "recognition over recall." A design may follow others in an organization, may be similar to others in a domain (like libraries or financial websites), or may inherit general patterns from the web. Users likely have learned from other sites and apps they use. Several patterns and principles developed in web and mobile persist across many systems, providing a good head start for IA design. In particular, Microsoft, Apple, and Google have done a lot to standardize patterns on their hardware and in their software designs, because they control so much of our digital ecosystem. However, IAs should be aware of the "me too" designs. Don't rely on others too much or too often, it may mean you are not innovating or addressing the real needs of your users.

> I need to design a mobile friendly, responsive website. Let's have the navigation roll-up into a hamburger menu on smartphones, we see that on a million sites.

7.5.5   Secondary Research

Secondary research is using the research published or shared by others to support your own work. Common sources for this include academic research and reports or whitepapers. Many academic researchers have published useful articles describing usability tests of faceted search interfaces, including empirical data, which we can use to help design features. Just like when a student writing term papers, we've have had good success citing research papers in IA design deliverables even as practitioners.

You must develop *critical evaluation skills* when using other's research to inform your work, particularly for sources like blogs and others found online. In the graduate courses that formed the basis of this book, we require that sources cited include some sort of *data to back up their assertions*—blogs and many web articles fall short here. Look into the context and reasoning behind articles—ensure they are relevant to your project and there is evidence to support the conclusions.

> I need to design a faceted search tool for the college's academic libraries. I'll look at some academic research papers by information science professors.
>
> We redesigned the college's website search 3 years ago, let's look through research deliverables from that project and see if there's anything relevant for our new project.

7.5.6 Primary Research

The *gold standard* for any project is conducting research and evaluation with the users of the system. Primary research puts the "focus on the user and not the product" (Barnum, 2010). In the previous methods there was no direct access to the user, they were not directly included in the design process. As we've learned, including users in the research process reduces the risk of building things that people do not want, or that do not work. In the medical field for example, it is not unheard of for doctors and nurses to refuse a system because poor usability hinders their ability to care. Quantitative measures and qualitative user quotes are extremely powerful when used to support design decisions.

> I need to design a tool allowing users to self-register for their courses, let's interview college students and find out how they register, and how we can improve the process.
>
> We just built a self-registration prototype, let's see how it performs with students.

7.5.7 Using the Framework

The research to design framework has three main uses. First, it can be used to structure information gathering activities, almost like a checklist of where to look for relevant facts or ideas when making design decisions. For example, conceptual designs could be roughly based on experience, theories, and patterns—and then evaluated with primary research. Or, in a resource-limited environment, when a critical piece of functionality is designed it should be based on primary research with theoretical support, while a minor part of the design could rely on less resource intensive principles and patterns.

Second, use the framework as a way to understand how and why design decisions were made. By recognizing the methods(s) used in the decision-making process, teams can mitigate the risk of design decisions that are not supported by a strong foundation. While primary research should be most persuasive, the other methods can provide substantial objective data to support a design. For example, designs that are supported only by theory are not necessarily poor but may be made stronger through triangulation, re-examining them with one or more of the other methods.

Finally, it is almost inevitable that in *a team environment, differences of opinions will arise*. Our framework is intended to support IAs in UX design "debates" (Bowles, 2010), and get to the best decision possible. People who work in the technology or business side of a project are unlikely to know the nuances of IA work, or the UX team members may have opposing viewpoints. Discussing the decision-making process, along with the strengths and weaknesses of the methods used and some relevant data, goes a long way towards building confidence in the final decision. We sometimes compare this to *showing your work* on math problems in primary school or citing your sources in a college paper.

7.6   Summary

Interaction design is about the intersection of users, interfaces and information. Designers are often called upon to create interactive interfaces, while IA work (even if just on the back end content and metadata) also has an impact on the user interface. Several principles have come about over the years that can be used (often alongside other principles and theories) to help guide interaction design—and this continues with the rapid rise of AI tools. The theories, principles, and patterns we've covered from Chap. 3 to here give us a toolkit to use in research and design, to help make the best decisions and design the most informed and human-centered experiences possible.

References

Alexander, C. (1979). *The timeless way of building*. Oxford University Press.

American Academy of Orthopaedic Surgeons. (2015). *Distracted walking*. American Academy of Orthopaedic Surgeons. https://orthoinfo.aaos.org/en/staying-healthy/distracted-walking/.

Amershi, S., Weld, D., Vorvoreanu, M., Fourney, A., Nushi, B., Collisson, P., Suh, J., Iqbal, S., Bennett, P.N., Inkpen, K., Teevan, J., & Horvitz, E. (2019). Guidelines for human-AI interaction. In *Proceedings of the 2019 chi conference on human factors in computing systems* (pp. 1–13).

Barnum, C. M. (2010). *Usability testing essentials: Ready, set... test!* Elsevier.

Bernsen, N. O., & Dybkjær, L. (2009). Multimodal usability. *Multimodal usability: Human-computer interaction Series*. Springer.

Bowles, C. (2010). *Winning a user experience debate*. UX Booth http://www.uxbooth.com/articles/winning-a-user-experience-debate/.

Budiu, R. (2016). *The power law of learning: Consistency versus innovation in user interfaces*. https://www.nngroup.com/articles/power-law-learning/.

Cooper, A. (2004). *The inmates are running the asylum: Why high-tech products drive us crazy and how to restore the sanity*. Sams.

Crampton-Smith, G. (2007). Forward: What is interaction design? In B. Moggridge, *Designing interactions*. MIT Press.

Fitts, P. M. (1954). The information capacity of the human motor system in controlling the amplitude of movement. *Journal of Experimental Psychology, 47*(6), 381–391. https://doi.org/10.1037/h00 55392

Gerchev, I. (2012). *Build your perfect interface with UI design patterns*. https://www.sitepoint.com/build-your-perfect-interface-with-ui-design-patterns/.

Gevelber, L. (2015). *Second-screen searches: Crucial I-want-to-know moments for brands*. Google. https://www.thinkwithgoogle.com/marketing-strategies/search/second-screen-searches-crucial-i-want-to-know-moments-for-brands/.

Hick, W. E. (1952). On the rate of gain of information. *Quarterly Journal of Experimental Psychology, 4*(1), 11–26.

Microsoft. (2016). *Inclusive 101 guidebook*. https://inclusive.microsoft.design/tools-and-activities/Inclusive101Guidebook.pdf.

Müller, H., Gove, J. L., Webb, J. S., & Cheang, A. (2015). Understanding and comparing smartphone and tablet use: Insights from a large-scale diary study. In *Proceedings of the annual meeting of the Australian special interest group for computer human interaction* (pp. 427–436).

Nielsen, J. (2000). *End of web design*. https://www.nngroup.com/articles/end-of-web-design/.

Norman, D. (1998). *The design of everyday things*. Basic books.

Nylander, S., Lundquist, T., & Brännström, A. (2009). At home and with computer access: why and where people use cell phones to access the internet. In *Proceedings of the SIGCHI Conference on Human Factors in Computing Systems* (pp. 1639–1642).

Pew Research Center. (2014). *Three Technology Revolutions*. http://www.pewinternet.org/three-technology-revolutions/.

Silver, K. (2007). *What puts the design in interaction design*. https://www.uxmatters.com/mt/archives/2007/07/what-puts-the-design-in-interaction-design.php.

Teo, Y. S. (2024). *What is interaction design?*. Interaction Design Foundation—IxDF. https://www.interaction-design.org/literature/article/what-is-interaction-design.

Tognazzini, B. (2001). *Maximizing human performance*. http://www.asktog.com/basics/03Performance.html.

Weisz, J. D., Muller, M., He, J., & Houde, S. (2023). *Toward general design principles for generative AI applications*. arXiv preprint arXiv:2301.05578. https://doi.org/10.48550/arXiv.2301.05578.

Weisz, J. D., He, J., Muller, M., Hoefer, G., Miles, R., & Geyer, W. (2024). Design Principles for Generative AI Applications. In *Proceedings of the CHI conference on human factors in computing systems* (pp. 1–22). https://doi.org/10.1145/3613904.3642466.

Wright, A. P., Wang, Z. J., Park, H., Guo, G., Sperrle, F., El-Assady, M., Endert, A., Keim, D., & Chau, D. H. (2020). *A comparative analysis of industry human-AI interaction guidelines*. arXiv preprint arXiv:2010.11761. https://doi.org/10.48550/arXiv.2010.1176.

Wroblewski, L. (2012). *Mobile first*. A Book Apart.

Yildirim, N., Pushkarna, M., Goyal, N., Wattenberg, M., & Viégas, F. (2023). Investigating how practitioners use human-ai guidelines: A case study on the people+ ai guidebook. In *Proceedings of the 2023 CHI conference on human*

Design Thinking to Systems Thinking

In the preceding chapters, we discussed the Human-centered design, Human-information behavior, user research, and design principles for digital products. Here we start to take a zoomed out perspective using the complementary methods of design thinking and system thinking. *Design thinking* is a problem-solving approach that's focused on empathy and human-centered solutions to specific, often tangible problems, by delivering products to the market (Lockwood, 2009). It was first popularized by the design consulting firm Ideo (http://ideo.com) and the Stanford Design School (the d.school; https://dschool.stanford.edu/). *Systems thinking*, which grew out of domains like system dynamics (Aronson, 1998; Forrester, 2010), is an analytical and knowledge building process that aims to understand the underlying structures, patterns, and dynamics governing the behavior of complex systems, and identify problem areas called leverage points so we can develop interventions that make the system perform better. Together these two ways of thinking provide a way to visualize, analyze and *think* about the challenges people face, and devise ways to improve them at the micro and macro levels.

Both design thinking and systems thinking are *human-centered* in that they are highly concerned with the people using a product or who are part of a system. They focus on understanding and solving problems, use iterative learning, and require creativity and an *innovation mindset* from practitioners. Design thinking is more targeted on a specific area or problem in a business context, while systems thinking takes a broader view and looks at how different areas connect and influence one another. By incorporating human-centered design (HCD), design thinking, and systems thinking UX designers and organizations can take a holistic view of their domain. There are not solid lines between the three methods, they're all part of a greater whole, which ultimately is creating systems to help improve

    121
W. Ding et al., *Information Architecture and UX Design*, Synthesis Lectures on Information Concepts, Retrieval, and Services, https://doi.org/10.1007/978-3-031-72138-0_8

Fig. 8.1 The human-centered mindset is central to human-centered design, design thinking, and systems thinking

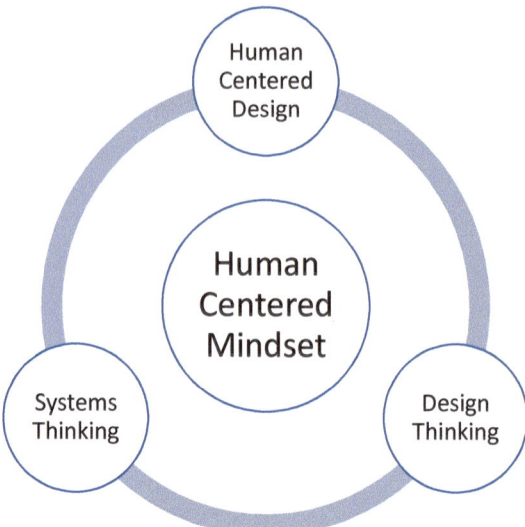

people's lives. Two important concepts, the human-centered mindset and zoom-in/zoom-out, help to connect these three areas.

8.1   Human Centered Mindset

A human centered mindset simply means looking at the users of a particular product or tool (as we typically do in human-centered design) and thinking about other people and processes and how it all fits together to help everyone involved. For example, if we create a highly usable university jobs website where students can go and add their resumes, that site is user-centered for the student. But, we also need to think about how an HR team will manage those resumes and reach out to students they think could be a good fit for their company. Without both sides of the equation, the student doesn't gain anything because the resume is never read, and the company gets little benefit from receiving resumes that are difficult to manage. Luckily for both the student and company in this example, the human-centered mindset helps us see both side and is helped by zooming out and taking a high-level view (Fig. 8.1).

8.2   Zoom In and Zoom Out

Zooming in and zooming out gives different perspectives on a system, helping us understand the complexities and challenges. When zoomed out we use a systems thinking lens to see how all of the different elements connect with one another. Zooming in with design thinking we start to inspect and improve a particular part of the system. And finally with human-centered design, we are looking directly at a product and learning how to make it highly effective for people to accomplish a discrete goal or task. Continuing the student job example, systems thinking looks at how we can create the processes to manage information so that HR professionals are able to find those great students. A design thinking project could be to improve the process by designing AI and automation technologies to augment HR tasks like scheduling interviews with students. Let's now take a deeper look at design thinking.

8.3   Design Thinking

Design Thinking is a process for creating new ideas for solving problems using a human-centered perspective. It incorporates the research methods, design principles, and user information behaviors. Organizations as like IBM, SAP, Uber, and many more use a design thinking framework to iteratively develop new products and services. The goal is to provide solutions by learning about people and their needs, and iterating through potential solutions, finding those that work (and those that don't work). Design thinking ensures we take a *structured and deliberate* approach to creating new products.

8.3.1   Definitions of Design Thinking

Definitions of design thinking center around a few main themes. It starts with a focus on people's needs and understanding their feelings and perception. Solutions must be technologically feasible and viable in a business. And, outcomes are the product of a methodological iterative approach.

- Tim Brown (2008), the CEO of IDEO, an influential design and consulting firm, defined design thinking as "a human-centered approach to innovation that draws from the designer's toolkit to integrate the needs of people, the possibilities of technology, and the requirements for business success."
- Rikke Friis Dam for the Interaction Design Foundation (2024) provides this definition: "Design thinking is a non-linear, iterative process that teams use to understand users, challenge assumptions, redefine problems and create innovative solutions to prototype and test. It is most useful to tackle ill-defined or unknown problems and involves five phases: Empathize, Define, Ideate, Prototype and Test."

There are many overlaps in the definition of design thinking and human-centered design. Remember to think of them as complementary to one another. The main take-away is that the focus remains on people's needs, and that you should expect to iterate and revisit ideas and assumptions throughout the process.

8.3.2 Design Thinking Process

In design thinking we start by gaining a deep understanding of our users, their needs, and what is meaningful to them, which is called empathy. This is the foundation for the design thinking approach. From here we define the problem we want to solve that will improve people's lives, and we ideate on a wide range of solutions. We use parts of each to craft a solution that is achievable from a technical standpoint and has business viability. Next, we move into prototyping and testing designs that solve those problems. We learn from each test and improve the solution each time. Finally, we make the design available to all users so they can enjoy the benefits of our work.

This should be familiar from the preceding chapters on human-centered design. Design thinking packages together the methods, techniques and processes in a framework to organize research and design projects. The roadmap provided by design thinking gives us a structure to run human-centered research and design projects in an organization, with structured inputs and outputs.

Design thinking is a very popular topic for organizations large and small, leading to several "flavors" or unique takes on the methods, which can become confusing for those new to the field. We like the short and simple "bootcamp bootleg" outline made available by the Stanford d.school at: https://dschool.stanford.edu/resources/design-thinking-bootleg. In our experience it's proven to be the most concise and simple way to approach design thinking, describing each step in the process and example methods to use for research, ideating, and prototyping. The d.school process (Fig. 8.2) clearly and simply illustrates the steps in design thinking. They define design thinking in five stages:

- Empathize: Understand users and their needs through user research (Chap. 4), we learn the context and motivations of users.
- Define: Create a point of view, define the problem we want to solve from a user perspective.
- Ideate: Think and develop a broad range of ideas to solve the problem. Go wide with possible solutions and give yourself the opportunity to think of creative or unexpected ideas.
- Prototype: Build a test system for users to interact with. Here we develop increasingly refined versions of a system (going narrow), improving each iteration using new learnings from testing. Prototypes can be paper, sketches, or more fully featured products.

Fig. 8.2 The design thinking process from stanford's d.school, with an Implement stage added

It's usually best to start with a very simple prototype, rather than spend a lot of time on something that may change substantially during testing, the next stage.

- Test: We evaluate the prototypes with users, gathering feedback and use this to iterate on our prototypes. In each round of testing, we learn more and more about the solution. Many times this is accomplished through usability testing. Testing will lead us to a product that we can launch to a general audience. Often this is considered a minimally viable product (MVP).
- An additional sixth step, Implement, is often added to the process to ensure we account for use of the design in production. We've added it here (Fig. 8.2) to show that the outcome of design thinking is a product that works in the real world.

The process is shown as a linear progression, but in practice it has many iterations and potential jumps backwards. In fact, a big challenge in explaining iterative design is illustrating the many steps back. An online image search for design thinking shows an array of illustrations, from the (too) simple to the (unreadably) complex. In the real world, the team frequently revisits previous work based on new learning and refines their ideas over time as new technologies or practices emerge.

8.3.3 Design Thinking in Practice

Let's look at how design thinking was used to help AirBnB when it was still a young startup. AirBnB is now a multi-billion dollar business with property listings around the world, but early in its history the company faced a widely-cited critical challenge that was solved with a design thinking approach: The company's growth had halted and they needed to find out why. The problem they uncovered was that photos potential customers viewed were often low quality. AirBnB co-founder Joe Gebbia defined this as potential customers would not pay to book rooms that they could not get to see clearly, "it actually wasn't a surprise that people weren't booking rooms because you couldn't even really see what it is that you were paying for." (First Round Review, 2015). To test the idea that better photos would result in more bookings, the team prototyped a solution by taking professional quality photos of properties and updated the property listings. The results of the test were a doubling of their then modest profits, however it resulted in the *first financial boost in the company in over eight months* and showed the benefits of a design thinking approach (First Round Review, 2015).

As instructors, we've seen students get confused when studying design thinking in part because they overthink it. Try to keep it simple. As the AirBnB example demonstrates, design thinking is just empathizing with users or customers and working in an interative way to provide a solution. In practice that can be difficult when there are pressures like deadlines or company leaders asking for changes. An approach that can help in mitigating these pressures is to position the design thinking projects as part of larger system improvements to demonstrate impact and connections to the greater whole. To do this we use systems thinking, which "unpacks the value chain within an organisation and externally. It complements design thinking: together they're a dynamic duo." (Tooley, 2021).

8.3.4 Systems Thinking

Like design thinking, systems thinking is a way of looking at complex problems. While design thinking focuses on the user experience and context while solving problems, systems thinking looks at connections and dependencies. Systems thinking is an approach to understanding complexity by "zooming out" and making explicit the relationships between the people and components. At its core, systems thinking helps us see the *connections between people, process, and technology,* and gives us a broad lens through which we can start to understand problems and areas of opportunity in new ways. It recognizes that *everything is interconnected* and that changes in one part of a system can have ripple effects throughout the entire system. This perspective allows for a more comprehensive understanding of complex systems, enabling us to identify patterns, anticipate consequences, and develop effective solutions that make the entire system work better.

Central to the concept of systems thinking is the idea of systems themselves. A system can be defined as a set of interconnected elements that work together to achieve a common purpose. These elements can include people, processes, organizations, resources, and more. By viewing the world through a systems lens, individuals can gain insights into how various elements interact and influence each other. Definitions from the systems thinking perspective emphasize the interconnected structure, organization, and notably the purpose of systems, whether they are natural or artificial (created by humans).

Meadows (2008) provides the following, emphasizing the purpose of elements and connections,

> A system isn't just any old collection of things. A system is an interconnected set of elements that is coherently organized in a way that achieves something. If you look at that definition closely for a minute, you can see that a system must consist of three kinds of things: elements, interconnections, and a function or purpose." (p. 11)

8.3.4.1   Definition of Systems Thinking

Definitions of systems thinking focus on visibility, perspective, and analysis. Here the main concepts are understanding and documenting. Rather than looking at elements or problems in isolation, we view the connections, relationships, and interactions of all the parts and consider the emergence of behaviors and outcomes from the interdependence of its components.

Peter Senge, in his book, The Fifth Discipline (1990) gives a thorough definition and overview of Systems Thinking, connecting it to the increasingly complex and information rich world we live in today:

> Systems thinking is a discipline for seeing wholes. It is a framework for seeing interrelation-ships rather than things, for seeing patterns of change rather than static "snapshots." It is a set of general principles—distilled over the course of the twentieth century, spanning fields as diverse as the physical and social sciences, engineering, and management…
>
> Today, systems thinking is needed more than ever because we are becoming overwhelmed by complexity. Perhaps for the first time in history, humankind has the capacity to create far more information than anyone can absorb, to foster far greater interdependency than anyone can manage, and to accelerate change far faster than anyone's ability to keep pace. Certainly the scale of complexity is without precedent. All around us are examples of "systemic break-downs"—problems such as global warming, climate change, the international drug trade, and the U.S. trade and budget deficits—problems that have no simple local cause. Similarly, orga-nizations break down, despite individual brilliance and innovative products, because they are unable to pull their diverse functions and talents into a productive whole (p. 99).

Additional definitions center on viewing the work as it is, and the connections, structures, and understanding.

- "Systems thinking is a way of seeing and talking about reality that helps us better understand and work with systems to influence the quality of our lives" (Kim, 1999, p. 2).
- "Systems thinking is a way of viewing the world as a cluster of interdependent systems. Think of it as a large machine in which one cogwheel drives the next" (Rutherford, 2021, p. 11)
- "Systems Thinking is the art and science of making reliable inferences about behavior by developing an increasingly deep understanding of underlying structure" (Richmond, 1994).
- "Systems thinking involves using a broader lens than user-centered design thinking. With systems thinking, in order to truly respond to large gnarly problems, you have to reach beyond a user, their problems, and a solution. The problem spaces are many, and a single solution does not exist." (Cababa, 2023, Chap. 3)

Systems thinking brings together many of the human-centered design skills, using the *creativity (art) and design principles (science)* that are inherent in Information Architecture and UX Design. Art and science are important skills needed for visualizing our systems so that we can identify areas to improve, using a technique called system mapping.

8.3.4.2   System Mapping

System mapping is a process used in systems thinking to create a visualization of a system, showing its components, relationships, and interactions. This helps in understanding, analyzing, and communicating the structure and dynamics of complex systems, it "helps practitioners gain clarity about an environment… [and] identify opportunities to gain leverage" (Omidyar, n.d.). The process includes defining the boundaries of the system, gathering data, drawing the map itself, and finally identifying leverage points—the areas on the map where an intervention can have an impact. Like design thinking, it is an iterative process where we revisit previous steps and gain clarity as new learning emerges. The Omidyar Network (https://www.omidyargroup.com/) and the System Mapping Academy (https://www.system-mapping.com/toolkit#toolkit) have both published open source mapping frameworks that give an excellent introduction to the step by step process of creating system maps. We use them as the foundation for our process below. But, before you get started mapping, two things are needed:

- **Build a team**: You will have a core team, these are the people who do the day to day work. Next, you'll want to identify extended team members, the subject matter experts who can lend their advice and insights, but who are not as heavily involved. Finally, you may want to identify others who may be called upon at just key moments, who Omidyar calls "participants," for their perspective at distinct points.
- **Collect data**: In addition to setting the team, you'll want to collect and review all the data and insights you already have. This will give your team the full range of knowledge you already possess and guide the beginning of the project.

Now that you have your team in place, and have reviewed the existing knowledge, you're ready to start mapping (Fig. 8.3).

Fig. 8.3 The system mapping team. Core team members do most of the work, with extended stepping in from time to time. Participants are called in more infrequently, at key moments

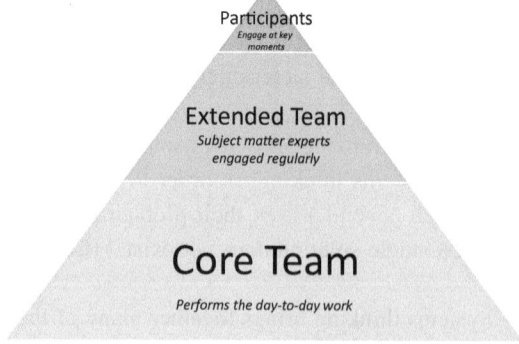

8.3.5 Mapping Process

Frame: The first phase, frame, is all about getting started, focused, and ensuring you have a vision for the mapping project. Here, you develop the primary research question, goals for creating a map, and the big problems to solve. You set the boundaries for the current work, because "our intervention to fix [the system] is much more thorough and targeted if we define well what we're trying to solve" (Rutherford, 2021. p. 22).

Explore: In the explore phase you determine the main outcome of the system. This is the key issue, representing your problem statement and research question. What is the main outcome of the system? Identify components: The individual parts such as people, machines, processes, or organizations. Develop groupings and themes: Collect the components into themes of similar items, like you would in an affinity diagramming exercise.

Map: Here we finally get to start drawing the map. Start by placing the key issue in the center and then the components in their groupings. Explore the relationships between the components and draw connections between them. Team members map the system's current state and identify "the most promising ways to potentially shift the system to a healthier state" (The Omidyar, n.d.) This can take several iterations to get right, and is where we can build shared knowledge by bringing together stakeholders who influence different parts of the system. We will see what are called feedback loops emerge. Feedback loops show the effect of relationships in a system and are important for analyzing how systems behave overtime. There are two types of loops, reinforcing loops, and balancing loops.

Reinforcing loops describe change in a component then results in further changes in the same direction, thus reinforcing or compounding the outcome. This can lead to positive or negative outcomes. For example, an app whose users provide a lot of useful restaurant reviews will attract users who want to read them, who will then leave reviews attracting even more users.

Balancing loops demonstrate a series of events that are self-regulating and achieve equilibrium. These are the stable parts of a system. A commonly used example is a thermostat controlling the temperature in a room. When the temperature drops below or goes above the setting, the thermostat turns on the heater or air conditioner, returning the temperature to its desired state.

Reflect: After your map is complete, you will want to "create your system story and get feedback" (System Mapping Academy, n.d.) from stakeholders and share the map widely. Like so many other things, this is an irritative process, you'll want to incorporate the feedback and update the map as needed. Crafting a system story during this phase will help develop deeper insights about our system, invite greater participation/feedback, and evolve our understanding. Note that while you are writing the story, you may refine your map based on new insights or thinking. Write down your story and include it when sharing the map.

Leverage: Next, you want to identify leverage points, those areas where an intervention can have a big impact and make the system better. As part of this process, you describe short term opportunities, what we might call quick wins. And, longer-term opportunities that will require more work, but have a greater influence on a "better future system" (System Mapping Academy, n.d.). We think of these longer-term opportunities as candidates for design thinking projects. While creating leverage points, you may also see opportunities to connect the current system to other systems, zooming out even further.

Deliver: And like in our design thinking process, the final phase is to deliver the innovations that improve the system. There is an opportunity to do two things: Deliver improvements to the current state system and eliminate problem areas, and drive innovation by introducing new products or services. And of course, as technology and society changes, we will need to adapt our maps to the changing environment (Meadows, 1999).

8.3.6   Benefits of System Mapping

System mapping can take several months and include many members of an organization. You will have mapped the current state, and using your analysis see areas to address problems (Cababa, 2023). After all this hard work, you will have:

- Shared understanding: Stakeholders at all levels have the same view and understand the system's structure and dynamics, not just their piece of it. Senior leaders and executives will gain new views into the connections between components and how they influence one another.
- Enhanced knowledge: By diving deep into the system, stakeholders will increase their knowledge which can lead to more informed decision-making and problem-solving. The people involved will see how their individual decisions influence other parts of the system.
- Leverage points: Clearly identified areas where a change can have an *exponential impact*. These are the points where an intervention (like a design thinking project) will improve parts of the system, contributing to its overall health.
- Project Roadmap Support: By surfacing the connections and leverage points, it supports project prioritization. Stakeholders can select the most promising areas to address and see the results of changes in future iterations.

8.3.7 System Mapping Case Study

Identifying, attracting, and hiring top job candidates is a critical function in human resources (HR). We call this system "talent acquisition." There is a vast array of technologies and techniques used in the system, with many technologies and tools for different groups across an organization. Despite everyone's best intentions, fragmentation the system can have serious implications. Almost every experienced professional has a story (or knows someone with a story) about a company not responding to a job application or encountering problems scheduling job interviews. The result can be a poor experience all around for people involved, and companies may miss out on that great employee. The system did not perform as it should for the job candidate while also failing the company hiring new employees. Alternatively, a streamlined and personalized experience can help attract the best job candidates and make the hiring process much more satisfying and efficient, and raise the company's profile with job seekers, hallmarks of a high performing system.

Phenom (http://phenom.com) is a global HR technology company that delivers single-platform solutions and hyper-personalized experiences for HR teams and candidates. This means integrating talent acquisition and management functions, providing UX design, AI, and Automations to help improve system performance, and delivering analytics to measure performance. Through consulting with hundreds of clients on their technology and processes, the Phenom team has identified many common challenges and opportunities and developed best practices for a highly effective talent acquisition system. System mapping proved to be a highly effective approach to diagnosing problems and sharing insights with clients to help improve their practices.

8.3.8 Mapping Process

Using a human-centered lens, the team researched and incorporated the experiences of all the people—both from the recruiting and hiring, and the job candidate perspectives. Open-source materials from the the Omidyar Group and System Mapping Academy's template (referenced above) were leveraged during the process. The objective of the effort was to:

- Analyze and visualize the current state talent acquisition processes.
- Enhance communication and collaboration between stakeholders.
- Pinpoint leverage points, where there were bottlenecks and inefficiencies.
- Identify opportunities to innovate.

The first step was framing the boundaries of the system to be mapped and defining the goals. In this case the team narrowed down the focus from all types of hiring, to only hiring what are called knowledge workers, who have jobs like nurses, IT professionals, and engineers. These roles are often critical to the success of an enterprise—it's hard to run a hospital without nurses—and finding the right candidates can be difficult, time consuming, and expensive. Next, stakeholder workshops, user interviews, and existing documentation was analyzed to identify the main element to improve, and the other elements, processes, and connections in the system. Here, the Core team involved the Extended team (mostly subject matter experts) on a regular basis and Participants, representatives from clients and customers who shared their experiences. By organizing this mountain of data in the frame stage, clear themes started to emerge.

The main element that emerged was *"The efficiency of hiring the best-fit candidate,"* meaning the time and effort it takes to make a great hire. The team then started drawing the map by placing the main element in the center and adding groupings of other elements, the areas where different people or teams will have the most responsibility. Next, connections were drawn between elements representing processes, loops, and information flows. This was a very iterative process, and included adding and refining as new information emerged, and validating with the extended team, and participants at key moments.

After the initial map was completed (Fig. 8.4), the team worked to identify leverage points, the areas where introducing changes will have a positive impact on the overall system. By identifying these leverage points, Phenom aims to make these areas exponentially better. Examples of leverage points identified include:

1. **Performance Accelerators**: Injecting human-centered AI, Automation, and Usability to greatly improve speed and efficiency throughout the system. These accelerators directly impact the users' day to day experience and influence the entire map.
2. **Brand Experience**: The candidate's impression of the organization as they begin the application process and continue their relationship with the hiring organization. Brand experience can be very important in attracting potential employees. For example, nurses and others in the medical field are often very interested in learning about their potential employer's commitment to outstanding health outcomes for patients.
3. **Interview and evaluation experience**: Scheduling interviews between the candidate and hiring team and evaluating the candidate. This point requires substantial coordination among the team and is helped immensely with AI technology.
4. **ROI and Planning Experience**: This involves the HR management team understanding the value of their talent acquisition process and tools, identifying areas to improve, and using data to forecast future needs. For example, if a large retailer wants to open an additional 100 stores, they can leverage historical data to make predictions on how to hire employees to staff the new locations.

8.3.9 Outcome

The map provides the Phenom team and its clients a clear view into how elements are connected in the talent acquisition system. Sharing the map with additional stakeholders provided the opportunity to identify contextually relevant areas for improvement unique

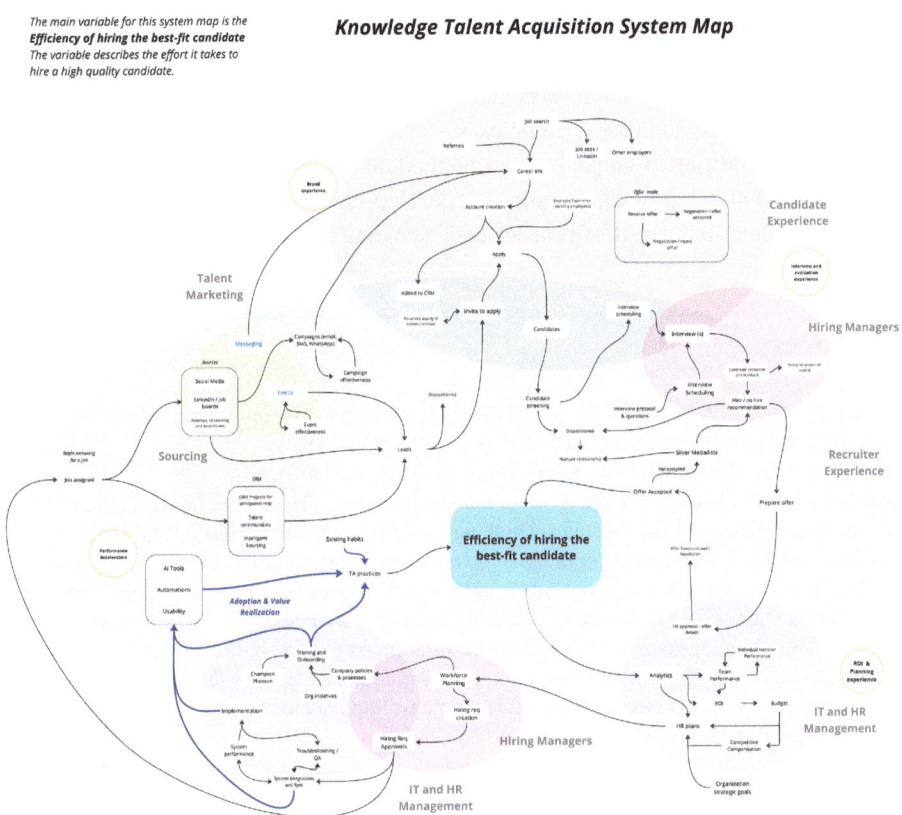

The main variable for this system map is the **Efficiency of hiring the best-fit candidate** *The variable describes the effort it takes to hire a high quality candidate.*

Knowledge Talent Acquisition System Map

Fig. 8.4 The knowledge talent acquisition system map. The map gives a clear view of the system for leaders and individual contributors. Taking a human-centered approach, the blue lines on this map highlight AI, automation, and usability components that directly influence the work practices of people in the system

to their organization. For example, one client reported they often hire candidates with about 70% of the skills needed, due to a very competitive job market. By using data from a candidate's evaluation in the interview process, the company has an opportunity to bridge the gap to the talent management system and create a learning plan for the new employee that fills the remaining 30% skills—a win for the employee who gains expertise and the employer who will have a more valuable contributor. Overall, systems thinking and system mapping has proven to be a powerful approach to building knowledge and providing insights contributing to increased performance and leading to new innovations.

8.4   Summary

In summary, design thinking focuses on solving specific problems through human-centered creativity and iteration, and systems thinking takes a more holistic approach to understanding and addressing complex systems' underlying structures and dynamics. While they have different emphases and methodologies, they complement one another, with design thinking providing tools for developing innovative solutions to specific challenges within the context of broader understanding fostered by systems thinking.

References

Aronson, D. (1998). *Overview of systems thinking.* https://community.mis.temple.edu/mis3534sec00 1spring2022/files/2021/12/Overview-of-Systems-Thinking.pdf.

Brown, T. (2008). Design thinking. *Harvard Business Review, 86*(6), 84.

Cababa, S. (2023). *Closing the loop: Systems thinking for designers.* Rosenfeld Media. https://www.amazon.com/Closing-Loop-Systems-Thinking-Designers-ebook/dp/B0BQQYQFDJ/.

Dam, R. F. (2024). *The 5 stages in the design thinking process.* Interaction Design Foundation—IxDF. https://www.interaction-design.org/literature/article/5-stages-in-the-design-thinking-process.

First Round Review. (2015). *How design thinking transformed Airbnb.* http://firstround.com/review/How-design-thinking-transformed-Airbnb-from-failing-startup-to-billion-dollar-business/.

Forrester, J. W. (2010). *System dynamics: The foundation under systems thinking.* Sloan school of management. Massachusetts Institute of Technology. http://static.clexchange.org/ftp/documents/system-dynamics/SD2011-01SDFoundationunderST.pdf.

Kim, D. (1999). *Introduction to systems thinking.* Pegasus Communications. https://thesystemsth inker.com/introduction-to-systems-thinking/.

Lockwood, T. (2009). *Design thinking.* Allworth Press.

Meadows, D. H. (1999). *Leverage points: Places to intervene in a system.* The Sustainability Institute. https://donellameadows.org/archives/leverage-points-places-to-intervene-in-a-system/.

Meadows, D. H. (2008). *Thinking in systems: A primer.* Chelsea Green Publishing.

Omidyar Group. (n.d.) *Systems practice.* https://www.omidyargroup.com/.

Richmond, B. (1994). *System dynamics/systems thinking: Let's just get on with it.* https://www.ise esystems.com/resources/articles/download/lets-just-get-on-with-it.pdf.

Rutherford, A. (2021). *Tools of system thinkers.* ARB Publications. https://www.amazon.com/Tools-Systems-Thinkers-Decision-Making-Problem-Solving-ebook/dp/B08S1QYHKT/.

Senge, P. M. (2006). *The fifth discipline: The art and practice of the learning organization.* Crown. https://www.amazon.com/Fifth-Discipline-Practice-Learning-Organization-ebook/dp/B000SEIFKK/.

System Mapping Academy. (n.d.). *System mapping toolkit.* https://www.system-mapping.com/too lkit#toolkit.

Tooley, C. (2021). What systems thinking actually means—And why it matters for innovation today. In *The world economic forum: Geneva, Switzerland.* https://www.weforum.org/agenda/2021/01/what-systems-thinking-actually-means-and-why-it-matters-today/.

IA in Practice

When discussing the Human Centered Design (HCD) methodology and processes, we touched on many aspects of the Information Architecture (IA) practice. In previous chapters, we also talked about the relationship between IA and Interaction Design (IxD) and other disciplines as the critical components of User Experience Design (UX).

Our focus here is on the collaborative dynamics of IAs or UX designers. We examine how they interact with various disciplines and stakeholders in projects, generate business value, and amplify their impact within the organization. We will navigate through three interconnected topics: Design Team Models, Design Culture, and Design Processes coupled with DesignOps. These components are pivotal in ensuring that design teams not only deliver scalable solutions but also operate with efficiency and success.

9.1 Design and Development Teams

9.1.1 Makeup of a User Experience Design Team

In addition to consulting firms and agencies, more and more organizations now have in-house design teams; UX is a growing area. Depending on many factors, the staff doing UX design work may have different titles and form various team configurations. Here, we introduce a typical model—the design staff coexists in a multidisciplinary team, usually called the User Experience team. The team is usually made up of the following:

© The Author(s), under exclusive license to Springer Nature Switzerland AG 2025
W. Ding et al., *Information Architecture and UX Design*, Synthesis Lectures
on Information Concepts, Retrieval, and Services,
https://doi.org/10.1007/978-3-031-72138-0_9

- User Researchers
- Information Architects (IAs)
- Interaction Designers (ID)
- Visual Designers
- Content Strategists
- Managers.

Figure 9.1 shows an example of typical UX team efforts with specialized roles, based on our own experience. While this was originally observed in traditional waterfall system development lifecycle, it is still applicable in Agile or other iterative processes. Along the timeline (x-axis), each role is involved with a different pattern of effort (y-axis). IAs tend to be involved in the earlier phase (visioning and conceptual design phases) while the ID picks up the work as it comes to the logical design phase all the way through documentation and post-design support. The IA and ID roles may be played by the same people on some UX teams (often called UX designers).

The User Researcher(s) gets involved in the project in a peak and valley pattern. When it is the time to conduct user research they have their peak time. Then they gradually taper off (valley) as others implement the findings. When a conceptual design is completed and ready for usability testing, the User Research peaks again. Another peak time occurs when the time comes to test a logical design prototype. The involvement of Visual Designers follows a different peak/valley pattern, with more involvement as IA efforts wind down.

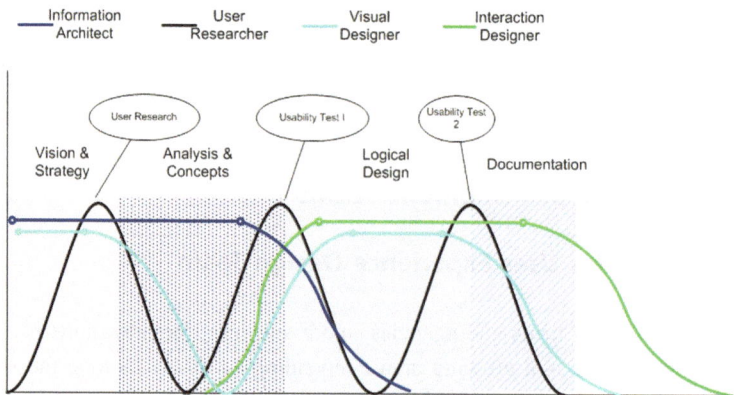

Fig. 9.1 User experience design disciplines peaks and valleys in the HCD process

9.1.2 Specialists, Generalists, and "T-Shaped" Professionals

There have been discussions on generalists and specialists based on different team models, including Jared Spool (Gabriel-Petit, 2009) and Institute of Data (2023). Generalists are the same people wearing multiple hats on the UX team, while specialists focus on their own disciplines and collaborate with specialists from other disciplines.

UX generalists possess a broad skill set that enables them to tackle various aspects of the UX design process. They are often involved in all stages of a project, from research and ideation to implementation and testing. UX specialists focus on developing deep expertise in specific areas of UX design. They are highly skilled professionals who excel in their chosen specialization, such as user research, interaction design, or visual design.

While it has been quite common to see IAs or UXers working in the Team of One (Buley, 2013), large organizations, as the design teams mature, tend to support specialists for several reasons: One being each role requires a different set of skills, and two being some roles (e.g., user researchers) need to maintain certain objectivity in assessing the design. We often use this analogy to describe the relationship between designers and researchers—if designers are attorneys rationalizing and presenting the case, researchers should play a judge role based on consumer insights and usability testing findings. This does not mean that designers are intentionally biased, but somehow may make certain unconscious assumptions along the way. When specialists work together, seamless collaboration and communication is important to the success of the team.

"T-shaped" professionals are people skilled in many areas, like generalists, but also have a depth of expertise in one area, like specialists. T-shaped individuals have "boundary-crossing" (Demirkan & Spohrer, 2015) skill sets. An example of this would be an expert ID who also can conduct research studies and work with content, and maybe even knows some programming or scripting. While T-shaped individuals can perform many roles, an equally important contribution is their ability to communicate effectively across disciplines. The script-savvy designer can help developers turn designs into working code by "speaking their language." In our lectures, we've also mentioned how IAs need to work with business stakeholders. That's another potential "T" proficiency, understanding skills needed to succeed in business.

9.1.3 Centralized Versus Distributed Organizational Models

In large organizations, there could be multiple design teams supporting different business lines. What is the ideal organizational model for the design teams? There are four business models to our knowledge. In some companies, there is a centralized UX group composed of individual UX teams for each business line. The UX group stands between the IT department and the business groups. In other companies, each UX group is part of the IT group supporting each business line. The way the third model works is that the each UX group is embedded within each business line. The fourth one is hybrid. There are pros and cons for each of the models.

- **Model 1, Centralized**: The centralized model allows the UX department to be the "Big Picture" keeper for the organization and makes it easier to push for enterprise design standards and guidelines, as well as design pattern sharing and reuse. It minimizes the learning curve for users (with coherent/consistent user experience). In addition, it allows for easier collaboration (across business lines) and best practice sharing. The UX team as a whole can have a stronger voice and higher visibility.
- **Model 2, Distributed or embedded across IT departments**: This model allows each UX team to focus on specific needs of each business line and also allows easier vertical resource management (the UX team and the IT development teams report to the same division/department). However, it is very easy to create isolated "design islands," which can be barriers for cross-organizational collaboration. Team A may not know about Team B's work.
- **Model 3, Distributed across the business lines (similar to Model 2)**: The only difference is design teams in Model 2 are more likely to have intimate technological knowledge.
- **Hybrid**, A combination of the above models.

How to choose the right model? It depends on many factors, such as the size and type of business, the communications process the business needs, and the competitive advantage in providing a stellar user experience. For small organizations, there may not be a sizable UX team. Outside consultants may take on much of the IA/UX efforts, or hybrid positions may be created, like a web developer who also handles UX tasks.

9.1.4   Maximizing the IA Impact

Because IA continues to be an evolving discipline, the value to the business may not be fully seen by some people. Therefore, selling IA is as important as creating successful IA designs. In almost every organization, IAs need to sell their ideas to people at different levels to justify their existence, demonstrate their value, and build up their reputation. In order to be successful, IAs need to pay attention to the following aspects:

- Understanding the business model
- Knowing your audience. You need to deal with different types of people including IT departments, business sponsors and stakeholders, and senior management (Fig. 9.2).

Fig. 9.2 Teams and roles in the HCD process

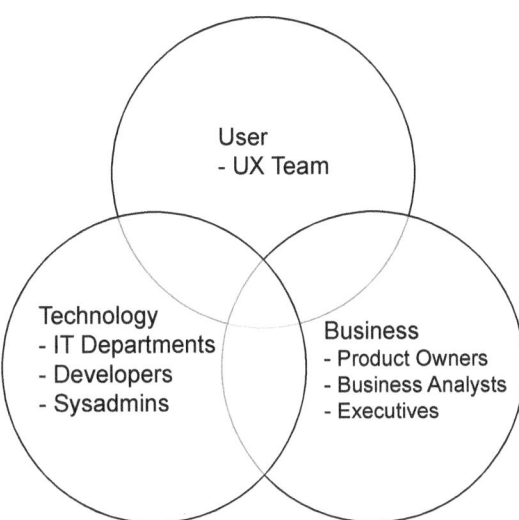

You need to understand their interests and needs and use their language when advocating for IA. For example, IT teams are interested in less rework and reusable code; business sponsors need to see how your designs are aligned with their business objectives. Senior managers and executives are ultimately interested in how UX will lower costs, increase sales, and improve employee productivity. You need to manage the HiPPOs (Highest-Paid Person's Opinions).

- Fighting the right battle. Do not expect that you can change the world overnight. Prioritize things and allow people time to have buy-ins. Also, keep in mind, you are not fighting against people, you are fighting for the right way to do things. At the end of the day, you need to have friends outside of the UX teams and disciplines instead of enemies, which leads to the next bullet point.
- Working on early adopters of HCD methodology and usability in the IT and business areas. The early adopters can then become UX champions to help spread the words and advocate the value.

9.1.5   Desired Competencies and Skill Sets for IAs

For students who are interested in becoming information architects, the following competency qualifications are commonly seen in IA or related job descriptions. This is also what the one of the authors required her team of IAs to have (Ding, 2009).

9.1.6   Being Strategic with Attention to Detail

Good IAs have the ability to work in great detail. But, at the same time, they can focus on broad strategic issues. The best information architects take user research, content analysis, business goals, and all of the other input information, and synthesize it into something that really works. They can see the big picture and keep an eye on all of the specific details.

9.1.7   Independent Thinker with Open Mind

Good IAs should demonstrate highly independent thinking. At the same time, they need to demonstrate flexibility to listen to others, be open to good ideas, and accommodate unpredictable needs.

9.1.8   Leader and Team Player

Any IA should be willing to take initiatives and leadership in any size or any type of effort. At the same time, they need to work closely with other team members and be willing to be a cooperative team player.

9.1.9   Problem Solver

A capable IA should be able to quickly digest a wealth of information thoroughly and make decisions effectively. Avoiding the trap of analysis paralysis is very important for anyone who is working in a fast-paced environment, or one with many competing demands.

9.1.10   Lifelong Learner with Passion for User Experience Design

Passion for UX is not just about liking what you do. It's about believing in the value of human-centered design and being committed to delivering the best possible experience for the users. This is what sets an excellent IA apart from a merely good one. A former product designer at Apple once shared her biggest learnings was to put passion to her work and her communication with others. The passion and excitement could influence people and move things forward (Pacheco, 2023). The passion also drives the designer to constantly learn new things, and stay updated with the latest trends, technologies, and best practices in the field.

9.1.11 Design Skills

Good IAs should be experts at converting user needs and business goals into appropriate design solutions. We consider this as the top competency of any good IAs.

We would like once again to differentiate "user wants" and "user needs." Good IAs and UX designers listen to the user, diagnose the problem, and then provide solutions. It is risky to simply give what the user or the business sponsor wants. We don't want to underestimate the value of visual design, but it is important to know that aesthetics alone cannot improve design effectiveness if the user needs are met. Visual design must be well integrated into the overall interaction flow.

And of course, UX designers should have in-depth knowledge in the following aspects we have covered earlier:

- Information organization and information retrieval knowledge.
- Human–Computer Interaction (HCI) knowledge including user cognitive characteristics and user behavior patterns.
- User research methods and usability engineering techniques.
- Knowledge about HCD methodology and system development process.
- Communication, marketing and project management skills.

As emerging technologies such as Ubiquitous Computing (Shepherd, 2024), Augmented Reality (AR), and Virtual Reality (VR) continue to evolve, the role of UX designers is becoming increasingly complex and vital. They are tasked with designing seamless interactions in a world where devices communicate effortlessly, crafting intuitive interfaces for voice-controlled AR glasses, and creating VR experiences that prioritize user comfort.

The rising of Generative Artificial Intelligence (GenAI) makes it increasingly important for UX designers to understand and utilize relevant AI tools to help themselves in their daily practice, as the usability guru Jacob Nielsen reminds the UX community of the urgency to embrace AI since it "holds the key to the future of UX" (Nielsen, 2023a, 2023b). Moreover, UX designers are responsible for ensuring ethical and personalized experiences through the judicious use of Generative AI. To meet these challenges, UX designers also need to collaborate with AI ethicists and other domain experts.

9.2   Design Culture and DEI

9.2.1   Building a Strong Design Culture

Good design culture can significantly impact the success of an organization's products and services. It allows organizations to create products that can better meet customer needs, increase customer loyalty, build competitive advantages, and boost operational cost-effectiveness. Here are some strategies to foster a strong design culture:

- Focus on user experience. A good design culture prioritizes user experience and is committed to researching to gain deep understanding of customer needs, motivations, and frustrations throughout the design process.
- Promote collaboration. Design is a collaboration process involving not only the UX team members but also multidisciplinary stakeholders, such as engineers, product managers, marketers and other groups. It's important to create an environment where everyone feels comfortable sharing their ideas and providing feedback. As a result, organizational silos get broken down via close collaboration and teamwork. Diverse perspectives are being considered to increase inclusion and reduce biases. In addition, collaborative culture helps people think about the big picture and focus on the interconnectedness of various elements (systems thinking as discussed in Chap. 8), therefore they can create more effective, user-centered, and sustainable design solutions. This also increases consistency and coherence of the overall user experience across products and allows product and design teams to learn from each other and reuse design solutions for similar problems. Finally, organizations that are invested in collaborative tools often find themselves benefiting from better teamwork, enhanced communications, increased productivity and better employee morale.
- Encourage continuous learning. As discussed earlier, passionate designers tend to be self-motivated to constantly learn new things and stay updated. From the UX leadership perspective, it is important to create a dynamic and empowering environment where continuous learning is not just encouraged, but becomes an integral part of the design team's DNA. They may help create a learning library to curate a collection of relevant design books, articles, conference presentations and online resources that are easily accessible to the entire team.
- Celebrating Wins and Learning from Failures: A core principle of Human-Centered Design lies in the iterative nature of the process. Successful design solutions are rarely achieved in a single stroke; they emerge from a continuous cycle of testing, learning, and refining. UX leadership plays a crucial role in fostering this environment by recognizing and celebrating successful design efforts that showcase the power of HCD, while also viewing failures as valuable learning opportunities that can inform future iterations (Aizlewood, 2018). This also helps the team shift the focus from achieving perfection to valuing the learning process.

9.2.2   Integrating DEI into Design Process

Diversity, Equity, and Inclusion (DEI) principles have been widely adopted in workplaces. In governmental environments, we often refer to it as DEI & A (for Accessibility). Embracing DEI &A in UX design is not merely moral imperative, it also constitutes a savvy business strategy. It fosters a range of perspectives, leading to a stronger understanding of the users/customers from all angles and more creative solutions with potential biases mitigated. By ensuring everyone feels valued and respected, DEI empowers the UX team and unlocks their full potential.

In the older editions of the book, we discussed the importance of accessibility and cultural sensitivity in UX design. Here we are highlighting more areas to integrate DEI.

- Diversify user research and inclusive design: Conduct extensive user research that includes a diverse range of target users, considering relevant factors like race, ethnicity, gender, sexual identity, age, cognitive or physical ableness, education level and socioeconomic status. This can help ensure that the needs of all users are considered in the design process.
- Representation in audio-visuals: Ensure diverse representation of users in design deliverables including photos, videos, illustrations, avatars or voice-driven products.
- Bias Checklists: Use checklists to help identify potential areas of biases in design deliverables. These checklists can serve as reminders to consider different aspects of DEI during the design process.
- UX team hiring and project team assembly: Champion diversity by recruiting UX team members from a variety of backgrounds. Ensure that a multitude of ideas and perspectives are not only valued but also integral to the design decision-making process. This approach fosters innovation and inclusivity, enhancing the overall user experience.

9.3   Agile, Lean UX and DesignOps

As we've discussed in previous chapters, IAs work in teams with other disciplines. In order to manage projects, several frameworks have been developed to help people work together when creating information spaces. For decades "Waterfall" was the only way to create software. Waterfall development favors heavy documentation, building to pre-established requirements, and delivering the final product at a predetermined deadline (which is often missed). We can easily see the problems with the waterfall approach: It does not incorporate change easily, which can mean delivering products that fail to meet rapidly changing user needs. To counter this, frameworks like Agile were created to help add flexibility in design and development. Below we present several frameworks that IAs are likely to encounter in practice.

9.3.1   Agile

Agile software development began in 2001 with the Agile Manifesto, as a reaction to previous waterfall methods (Beck et al., 2001). Agile prioritizes incremental development, responses to changing priorities and technologies, and collaboration with users (called customers). Pivoting and changing direction as new information becomes available, while incrementally delivering features and functionality is fundamental. An important role in Agile teams is the "Product Owner," who is responsible for the overall vision of a product and prioritizes features for design and development, balancing the three components of user-centered design: Business, Technology, and Users. IAs and Product Owners work closely together.

The Agile manifesto is found at https://agilemanifesto.org/:

We are uncovering better ways of developing

software by doing it and helping others do it.

Through this work we have come to value:

Individuals and interactions over processes and tools

Working software over comprehensive documentation

Customer collaboration over contract negotiation

Responding to change over following a plan

That is, while there is value in the items on

the right, we value the items on the left more.

Often Agile is practiced using a "scrum" process in which features are delivered at the end of relatively short "sprints." Sprints are development cycles typically lasting between one and four weeks. At the end of each sprint users are able to interact with the new features, affording IAs the opportunity to inspect the usability of a live system and plan changes for the next iteration. Another popular flavor is "Kanban," which focuses on work in progress, and is less structured than scrum.

In Agile scrum, there are a few points for IAs to consider:

- **Sprint 0**: This is the planning phase before development starts. Substantial user research often happens in this phase.
- **Sprint Ahead**: Because Agile sprints happen in time-bound segments, IAs often work one or two sprints ahead of developers, preparing wireframes and prototypes for them to code.
- **Demos**: These are the days where the final working features are demonstrated on the last day of the sprint. IAs can inspect how well the work was implemented, and plan any needed adjustments.

- **Spikes**: Agile comes from the software development world and is aimed at producing working code. Spike tasks are for research and information gathering activities, rather than producing code.

An important component of Agile that aligns well with IA/UX is the principle of "customer collaboration over contract negotiation," meaning collaborating with users (customers) to find what features should be built, over building only those features determined at the outset of a project. This is a big difference from waterfall in that the team can change course—the final product may be changed from what was first conceived. For example, let's say a library is creating a new website, and they learn that social book reviews are very important to their patrons, even though it was not a priority feature in the initial project plan. Rather than ignore what they learned and build to the "contract," the Agile team can instead add customer reviews as an early feature. Although it may sound simple to just make the change, in reality there may be a big cost and impact on time. Agile helps expose these costs and time commitments, so the team (business, technology, and UX) can come to a shared understanding of the investment needed to deliver, and how it may be prioritized against other work. IAs with their research and design skills can have a big role in helping Agile teams pivot and learn about features, working with other stakeholders and users. The spirit of collaboration and including users is followed in all of the frameworks we discuss below.

9.3.2 Lean UX

Lean UX (Gothelf & Seiden, 2013) is based on three foundations: Design thinking, Agile software development, and the Lean startup method (Ries, 2011). Borrowing from these areas, the aim of Lean UX is to have collaborative teams constantly testing new features with users, and learning from their feedback. Eric Reis first proposed lean methodology as a way of developing new products and business ideas. Lean relies on learning from customers and users, rapidly validating ideas, and evolving products and solutions. Each idea is seen as a hypothesis to be tested, as quickly and efficiently as possible. IAs can adopt Lean principles (Lean UX) as a way to structure projects, gather user feedback, and guide the iterative design of information spaces.

The Lean UX process starts with declaring assumptions, developing a problem statement, and transforming assumptions into a hypothesis—how we think we can solve the problem. Hypotheses in Lean UX include creating personas and describing features and outcomes. Next, a Minimum Viable Product (MVP) is created, which is often a functioning prototype of a system or feature, and is analogous to conceptual designs in the processes we've described previously. Finally, the MVP is tested with users, and the feedback used to plan the next steps. Lean often uses a "canvas" to plan process and work, an example of a Lean UX Canvas is available from Jeff Gothelf's website: http://www.jef fgothelf.com/blog/leanuxcanvas/.

9.3.3   Rocket Surgery Made Easy

Steve Krug, an influential usability researcher and author, suggests "a round of testing once a month, with three users" (Krug, 2010, p. 23). This method of small, regularly scheduled rounds of testing helps to identify usability issues that can be fixed in the next round of development. Krug's method can be adapted into existing design/development cycles, and he suggests modifying the number of participants if testing takes place more frequently. However, Krug cautions that testing should not take place less than once a month, the point being that continuous feedback from users is necessary to find and fix usability problems.

In summary, Agile, Lean UX, and other development frameworks like GV Design Sprints discussed earlier in Chap. 3, put an emphasis on user research in an iterative process. It proves to be beneficial to integrate UCD into the organization's enterprise system development processes, more specifically, it leads to reduced development costs through early user feedback, improved user experience through continuous refinement based on user needs, and increased team collaboration.

9.3.4   DesignOps

DesignOps, short for Design Operations, is a set of practices and principles that aims to streamline the effectiveness of design teams. The ultimate goal is to build an environment in which designers can strive. The Nielsen Norman Group defines DesignOps as the orchestration and optimization of people, processes, and craft in order to amplify design's value and impact at scale (Kaplan, 2019).

Over the years, UX and IA fields have been experiencing accelerated growth. Designers are increasingly involved in strategic conversations and their value is widely recognized within their institutions. Meanwhile, this has led to an increased workload, leaving designers with less time for their primary tasks of designing and researching. In addition, the complexity of design contexts has also increased, with many organizations adopting embedded team models for specific products or projects. As discussed earlier in this Chapter, the challenges facing this type of team structure could result in a lack of connection among designers spread across different teams and various locations.

There have been various definitions of DesignOps. Krawczyk (2024) states that there are four levels of DesignOps maturity in an organization. Ranging from level 1 to level

4, DesignOps can be a practice, a role, a team or a department. Here we are mainly discussing DesignOps as a user-centered approach to addressing the evolving demands and complexities of the design field:

- **Optimizing the Design Team**: DesignOps helps ensure the design team has the necessary skills and expertise to tackle projects effectively; defining roles and responsibilities to ensure clear roles and ownership within the design team and prevent confusion and wasted effort; encourages open communication and collaboration between designers, developers, product managers, and other stakeholders.
- **Streamlining Design Workflows**: DesignOps defines efficient workflows for common design tasks like ideation, user research, design handoffs, and prototyping. It also standardizes tools and templates so that team members use consistent design tools and templates to promote efficiency and minimize compatibility issues. DesignOps also helps identify repetitive tasks that can be automated using design automation tools, freeing up designers' time for more creative endeavors.
- **Amplifying Design Impact**: DesignOps establishes metrics to track the effectiveness of the design process and the impact of design decisions on the overall product. It also helps the design team adapt and scale their processes to handle larger projects and a wider range of design needs.

9.4 Summary

IAs today are working on larger and larger projects that seem to become more and more complex. Across many industries and domains, a focus on value of user experiences is increasing. In order to improve efficiency and be more user-focused, design and development teams are structured in ways that bring together various disciplines and help them work towards a common goal, but there is no one-size fits all approach. Although IAs are highly involved in just some parts of a project, their work is instrumental throughout the entire process. UX team members may be generalists, with expertise across domains or specialists who focus on one area. Those who can combine generalist and specialist traits (T-shaped) can be quite valuable to a team.

Strong design culture prioritizes inclusive user experience and teamwork. It thrives on continuous learning, celebrating wins, and learning from failures. This is best achieved with a diverse team.

As the HCD principles and UX designers are well integrated to Agile and other iterative system development processes, the UX teams' organizational impact has been widely recognized. Accordingly, DesignOps are being adopted to help orchestrate and optimize UX processes, workflows, and design infrastructure and resources to handle more complex projects and wider range of design needs and to achieve operational excellence.

References

Aizlewood, J. (2018). Learning from failure in the design industry. https://jonaizlewood.com/writes/learning-from-failure-in-the-design-industry.

Beck, K., Beedle, M., Bennekum, A. van, Cockburn, A., Cunningham, W., Fowler, M., Grenning, J., Highsmith, J., Hunt, A., Jeffries, R. and Kern, J., & Thomas, D. (2001). *Manifesto for agile software development*. http://agilemanifesto.org/.

Buley, L. (2013). *The user experience team of one: A research and design survival guide*. Rosenfeld Media.

Demirkan, H., & Spohrer, J. (2015) Point of View: T-Shaped Innovators. https://www.researchgate.net/publication/282397832_Point_of_View_T-Shaped_Innovators.

Ding, W. (2009). *Marriott IA team mission statement*. Internal Presentation.

Gabriel-Petit, P. (2009). Specialists versus generalists: A False Dichotomy? https://www.uxmatters.com/mt/archives/2009/02/specialists-versus-generalists-a-false-dichotomy.php.

Gothelf, J., & Seiden, J. (2013). *Lean UX: Applying lean principles to improve user experience*. O'Reilly Media, Inc.

Institute of Data. (2023). *Exploring the difference between UX generalists and UX specialists*. https://www.institutedata.com/us/blog/ux-generalists-and-ux-specialists/.

Kaplan, K. (2019). *DesignOps 101*. NNGroup. https://www.nngroup.com/articles/design-operations-101/.

Krawczyk, B. (2024). *What is DesignOps? The essentials of DesignOps*. LogRocket https://blog.logrocket.com/ux-design/what-is-designops/.

Krug, S. (2010). *Rocket surgery made easy: The do-it-yourself guide to finding and fixing usability problems*. New Riders.

Nielsen, J. (2023a). *AI versus metaverse: Which is the 5th generation UI?* https://www.uxtigers.com/post/ai-vs-metaverse.

Nielsen, J. (2023b). *UX needs a sense of urgency about AI*. https://jakobnielsenphd.substack.com/p/ux-needs-a-sense-of-urgency-about.

Ries, E. (2011). *The lean startup: How today's entrepreneurs use continuous innovation to create radically successful businesses*. Crown Books.

Pacheco, A. (2023). *What I learned as a product designer at apple*. UXMag. https://uxmag.com/articles/what-i-learned-as-a-product-designer-at-apple.

Shepherd, S. (2024). *Ubiquitous computing in UX discipline*. https://mockitt.wondershare.com/ui-ux-design/ubiquitous-computing.html.

The Future of IA/UX Design

10

The future is already here—it's just not very evenly distributed—attributed to the author William Gibson.

Over the past nine chapters we have discussed key concepts of Information Architecture (IA) and UX Design, research methods and tools, design and design implications, and IA applications in enterprises, web, mobile, and AI. Coming to this closing chapter, let's take one more look at the domain itself, with a particular curiosity of its future in mind. What are the global influences driving design around the world? What's the state of the online world today? What are the future trends? In this chapter, we will discuss these questions and look to the future.

10.1   Global Considerations

As the internet brings people around the world closer and closer together, designers have more opportunities to create systems for a global audience. Particularly in developing regions, design priorities may be different due to a reliance on mobile devices or other factors (some areas went from no internet directly to mobile only, bypassing much of web1.0 and web2.0). While global IA covers a lot of topics, in this section we focus on the user experience strategy for organizations that interact with their users in multiple languages/cultures, different countries, or in a combination of both. People from different

© The Author(s), under exclusive license to Springer Nature Switzerland AG 2025
W. Ding et al., *Information Architecture and UX Design*, Synthesis Lectures
on Information Concepts, Retrieval, and Services,
https://doi.org/10.1007/978-3-031-72138-0_10

cultures and countries have different value systems and cognitive styles, which may lead to different expectations of user experience and usability. Companies and businesses with global services and products need to pay close attention to those factors so that they can design their user interfaces to best meet the user needs.

10.1.1 Makeup of the World's Internet Users

The International Telecommunication Union (ITU), part of the United Nations, estimates that in 2023 there were 5.4 billion internet users, representing 67% of the global population (Table 10.1), an increase of 3.5% from the year before (2023a). That's a lot of people to design for, each of whom have their own unique characteristics while also sharing similarities with a larger group.

There also remains a wide range of internet use by country. The World Bank (2024) estimates that some countries such as Saudi Arabia and The United Arab Emirates have 100% of their population online (as of 2022), while others are 10% or even lower. In general, more developed nations will have a higher percentage of their populations online. In the United States, the Pew Research Center (2024) reports 95% of people using the internet, with 80% having a broadband connection at home. Compare this to 52% online and just 1% with home broadband in 2000.

These metrics help IAs and businesses develop strategies and tactics on how to deliver information. In areas where there is high Internet penetration, you can expect to see more digital services. You may also expect that the population is more digitally savvy and expects more from the systems they interact with. User interface, design and visual design, and the whole user experience, will have to meet the expectations of this audience. We could also expect that this population is familiar with the main design patterns discussed in chapter seven.

Table 10.1 Regions and percent of population using the internet (International Telecommunication Union, 2023a)

Region	Percent of population using the internet (2023) (%)
World	67
Africa	37
Americas	87
Arab States	69
Asia–Pacific	66
Commonwealth of independent states (CIS)	89
Europe	91

Table 10.2 Top languages on the internet (W3 Techs, 2024)

Language	Percent of websites (%)
English	49.9
Spanish	5.8
German	5.4
Japanese	4.9
French	4.3

10.1.2 Languages Used on the Internet

English is the predominate language on the internet, with estimated 49.9% of websites today (W3 Techs, 2024). No other language comes close to its use. English is so heavily represented because the internet was invented in English-speaking countries, many early adopters spoke English, the US is a global leader in tech and innovation, English is the world's most commonly taught second language, and it is "used as a common language for international business, academia, and diplomacy" (Internet Society Foundation, 2024). Table 10.2 shows the top six languages used on the internet, as of June 15, 2024. Although many websites are in English, IAs and designers should still work to make sure systems are available in the necessary languages, and work towards internationalization and localization when appropriate.

10.1.3 Mobile Use

Designers should be aware of the predominant devices used, and in many cases mobile is the leader. More than three quarters of the world's population own a mobile phone (Table 10.3), and mobile phones are the most common way people access the internet. (International Telecommunication Union, 2023b) However, we must be aware of context. It is unlikely (today) a smartphone will be used to access a complicated SaaS online office tool, in which case designers should try to offer a mobile friendly version, with the top tasks supported.

In these highly mobile societies IAs and UX designers will likely be called upon to develop mobile friendly applications, and can expect to take a mobile first approach. Additionally, when expanding to a new region, organizations should be aware of the top devices used to ensure that their applications and services meet the users where they are. For example, in many parts of the world, Android smartphones are predominant, however in the United States, Apple's iPhone is the leader. If a US-based company wants to expand, they should be aware of this difference and plan their design and development accordingly. WeChat and WhatsApp have achieved high market penetration around the

Table 10.3   Mobile phone ownership (International Telecommunication Union, 2023b)

Region	Percent aged 10 or older with a mobile phone (%)
World	78
Africa	63
Americas	88
Arab States	82
Asia–Pacific	75
Commonwealth of independent states (CIS)	93
Europe	93

world, but similar to Android, they are not leaders in the United States. When thinking about integrating information spaces, the global IA should be aware of these distinctions.

10.1.4 The Need for Internationalization and Localization

Globalization makes it possible for companies to gain significantly bigger portions of sales outside of their domestic markets. Nike sells its products in over 100 countries, and McDonalds also operates in over 100 countries. A key to success for those multinational companies is understanding local markets, and positioning products and services. It is equally important to understand and meet the needs of employees in different regions and countries to boost collaboration and improve job productivity.

> People with different cultural backgrounds think and behave differently. Examined closely, these differences go way beyond speaking and writing in different languages. Cultural differences are present in values and attitudes, social relationships, communication styles, visual preferences, and cognitive styles. All of these potentially affect the design of highly usable and satisfying user interfaces for users from different cultures. (Plocher et al., 2021, p. 162)

All of this points to a focus on internationalization and localization for websites, apps, and intranets. While *internationalization* (I18N) is about designing an application or website so that it can be adapted to various languages and regions without engineering changes, *localization* is the process of adapting through language, content and design to reflect local cultures. Many subtle or significant differences need to be taken into consideration in cultural preferences, language, tradition, and religion. The next section introduces how cross-cultural theories help guide the localization of website designs.

10.1.5 Cross-Culture Theories and Localization

Here, we introduce two sets of well-known cross-culture theories that can be used to guide the user experience strategies for localization. One is Hall and Hall (1989) theory about High Context (HC) versus Low Context (LC) culture, and the other is Hofstede's Cultural Dimensions framework (1984). In addition, empirical studies also show evidence that people from different cultures interpret usability differently. Even the way they organize information is different (Frandsen-Thorlacius et al., 2009; Morville, 2003; Plocher et al., 2021).

10.1.6 High Context Versus Low-Context Culture Types

Hall and Hall (1989) states that all cultures can be situated in relation to one another through the styles in which they communicate. In LC cultures, such as France, North America, Scandinavian Countries, and German-speaking countries, LC communication occurs predominantly through *explicit* statements in text and speech—the mass of the information is vested in the explicit code. As such, most of the information must be in the transmitted message in order to make up for what is missing in the context. High-Context cultures, including Japan, Arab Countries, Greece, Spain, Italy and England, involve *implying* a message through that which is not spoken; messages include other communication cues such as body language, eye movement, paraverbal cues, and the use of silence. HC communication is identified as indirect, ambiguous, maintaining harmony, reserved and understated. In contrast, LC communication is identified as direct, precise, dramatic, open, and based on feelings or true intentions.

The HC and LC theory has been applied to guide international website design. By studying the global fast food chain McDonald's country-specific websites, Würtz (2005) found a set of differences among local websites of the same company.

- Websites in HC tend to use more animated effects than those in LC;
- Low-Context websites are expected to be consistent in their layout and color schemes, whereas pages in High-Context websites are expected to be diverse.
- Opening of links in the same browser windows in LC websites is in contrast to the HC Asian websites where new pages would open in new browser windows, giving the visitor a multitude of starting points for further website navigation.

10.2   Hofstede's Five Cultural Dimensions

10.2.1 Overview of the Five Dimensions

Based on his five years of intensive research with hundreds of IBM employees in 53 countries, Dutch cultural anthropologist Geert Hofstede (1984) identified five cultural dimensions. He rated all the 53 countries on indices for each dimension, normalized to values (usually) of 0 to 100. The five dimensions of culture are the following:

- Power-distance: The extent to which the less powerful members of institutions and organizations within a country expect and accept that power is distributed unequally.
- Collectivism vs. individualism: Individualism pertains to societies in which the ties between individuals are loose; everyone is expected to look after themselves and immediate family. Collectivism pertains to societies in which people from birth onwards are integrated into strong, cohesive in-groups, which throughout people's lifetime continue to protect them in exchange for unquestioning loyalty.
- Femininity vs. masculinity: Masculinity pertains to societies in which social gender roles are clearly distinct; femininity pertains to societies in which social gender roles overlap.
- Uncertainty avoidance (UA): The extent to which people feel anxiety about uncertain or unknown matters. Cultures with high UA tend to have more formal rules, and focus on tactical operations rather than strategy. People seem active, emotional, and even aggressive. By contrast, low UA cultures tend to be more informal and focus more on long-range strategic matters than day-to-day operations. These cultures tend to be less expressive and less openly anxious; people behave quietly without showing aggression or strong emotions; people seem easy-going and relaxed.
- Long vs. short-term orientation: Long-term orientation is also called "Confucian dynamism." Persistence (perseverance), ordering relationships by status and observing this order, thrift and having a 'sense of shame' are the dominant values. The values of perseverance and thrift are future oriented and more dynamic while the short-term values are more static, being past and present oriented.

10.2.2 Implications of Cultural Dimensions on Design

Chessum et al. (2023) in a study of search user interfaces report the potential for Hofstede's dimensions to inform and enhance the user experience and recommend additional research in this space. When using cultural dimensions as a framework to analyze websites, researchers (Frandsen-Thorlacius et al., 2009; Marcus & Gould, 2000) reported the following distinctive user experience focuses from different cultures. LC cultures tend to have low scores in Power Distance and Uncertainty Avoidance, and more Collectivism oriented; and vice versa. Both LC/HC theory and Uncertainty Avoidance dimension can well explain why Europeans expect compact webpages with a few precise links, while many Asian consumers on high-bandwidth networks expect results as screens full of colorful content.

10.2.3 Guidelines for Global IA and UX Design

There are two common ways to localize information systems:

- A surface-level translation of language and jargon to reflect the conventions of the target audience.
- A deeper aesthetic change, altering images, colors, logic, functionality and branding to conform to the target audience on a cultural level (Sun, 2001).

Below are some specific guidelines for globalization:

- Pay Attention to Language Details: Translation is by no means straightforward. Sometimes, there is no direct mapping between languages and people in different cultures interpret words/meanings differently. For example, the word 'flat' in Nebraska is not the same as a 'flat' in London.
- Text Swell: The difference between the width of text between various languages. Typically, German translations require 30% to 40% more space than English. Sometimes, while some English labels or phrases can fit in one line, in German it would require text wrapping. Be aware of left-to-right and right-to-left translations.
- The Combination of Languages and Countries: Most countries speak multiple languages and some languages are spoken in multiple countries. Do not assume that there is one to one mapping between each country/region and the official language of the country.
- Language options need to be obvious and easy to find. Otherwise, most people would assume there are no such options. List choices in the target language, not English.
- Avoid Using Non-Universal Symbols and Iconographies: Be sensitive to the customs and practices of other cultures. For example, the 'okay' sign (index finger and thumb together forming a circle) is considered obscene in Brazil, while the thumbs-up gesture in Iran is highly offensive.
- Colors Have Cultural Significance: It is imperative that you do your homework before you choose colors for your international website (Iler, 2007). For example, black in Western culture is the color of mourning; not so in Asia, where white signifies death.

- Understanding Cultural Subtlety: In Chinese culture, almost all names have some meaning, especially for company names or trademarks. Company names are often considered as the equivalent of their brands.
- Beware of Users' Environmental Situations: For example, multiple family members may share one account in collectivism cultures (e.g., in Vietnam). People may sit side by side to browse the Web together. Under these circumstances, system features like shared accounts and co-browsing should be taken into consideration.
- Supporting Global eCommerce: Ensure that the preferred payment and delivery methods are provided for users.
- Platform: Understand the primary platforms in each country or region. For example, much of the world uses WhatsApp, while it has not caught on as heavily in the United States.

Global design is growing in importance as more people around the world are connected. Western/English speaking is the predominant paradigm for many today, but IAs should be aware that their work can reach a worldwide audience. Designing for a global product is challenging, however with new web-based technologies, user research and design efforts can be coordinated around the globe from a central location, connecting IAs with a new global audience.

10.3   The Future of IA and UX

Let's take one more look at IA and UX design itself, with a particular curiosity of its future in mind. What are the trends in IA? What are the relationships between UX design and research? Let's discuss these questions and look to the future of information architecture.

10.3.1 Key Challenges

The information technology environment has constantly changed over the last two decades. While IA and UX design grew rapidly from a need to create more usable websites, the field now includes all manner of devices and products. This expansion of the roles brings new opportunities as well as new responsibilities and challenges that come with the opportunities. In the following, we briefly discuss some of the new challenges.

10.3.2 UX Community

Before we get to the challenges, let's take a look at some of the resources we have to help meet them. UX has a strong community that includes professionals in IA, human factors, visual design, and many more. Information and learning resources are freely shared on blogs and websites, and in-person or remote meetups. Below are some resources we've found helpful.

MeasuringU: http://www.measuringu.com/blog.php

A extremely valuable resource for learning the quantitative side of IA and UX, provides many excellent insights into standardized questionnaires and usability measures, like SUS and UMUX-Lite. We've cited research from Sauro and Lewis, leaders at this organization, several times.

UX Tigers—Jakob Nielsen's New UX Articles https://www.uxtigers.com/ and NN/g—Nielsen Norman Group: https://www.nngroup.com

This is an absolute thought leader in the field of HCI, usability, user experience design, and information architecture. We've cited this source throughout our book.

ACM—The Association for Computing Machinery: http://www.acm.org

The ACM is the world's largest educational and scientific computing society and supports research in our field. The special interest group SIGCHI has local chapters around the world, https://archive.sigchi.org/chapters/; and the ACM digital library is an invaluable resource for academic research, https://dl.acm.org/.

Interaction Design Foundation: https://www.interaction-design.org/blog

A large collection of UX design resources, with articles by top names in the field.

IxDA: The Interaction Design Association: http://ixda.org

IxDA supports professionals in the Interaction Design community, with a goal of advancing the human condition through better design.

Laws of UX: https://lawsofux.com/

An engaging resource with concise descriptions of many laws and principles in our field.

UX Magazine: https://uxmag.com/

An online resource and community with articles and resources for UX professionals.

World IA Day: http://worldiaday.org

World Information Architecture Association (WIAA) hosts World IA Day, the one-day annual celebration held in dozens of locations across the globe.

These resources and many more help the new and experience IA alike learn and keep their skills up to date. There are also countless UX books and conferences to help you on your journey. We're fortunate to be part of a UX community where so many freely share their knowledge to help others.

While visual design and interaction design have long been a part of human computer interaction departments, more recently universities have started offering degrees in the User Experience field. A search for user experience degrees returns hundreds of options.

Drexel University (n.d.) for instance, offers a Master's in Human–Computer Interaction & User Experience that "prepares students to create technologies that support and complement human needs and abilities in contexts such as work, wellness, home, entertainment and artistic expression."

In addition to university courses, many additional firms like IDEO and Google offer certificates in user experience and related disciplines. Design thinking, in particular, has become a very popular executive education, topic, and systems thinking is similarly taught in business programs. These certificate programs recognize that many graduates have a diverse set of skills and overtime may see the need to focus on a particular area to solve business problems. Through the combination of the community, university, courses, and certificate programs IAs and UX designers are well equipped to face the challenges we discuss next.

10.3.3 Findability and Cross-Channel/Ubiquitous Access

Findability has long been established as an essential task for IA (Morville, 2005), and remains a challenge. As people move to a multi-device experience and use Generative AI (GenAI) powered agents (like search or chatbots), information needs to be useful in multiple contexts. Content created in one context may be needed in another. Content may be used and combined to create new content through large language models and GenAI. As we discussed in chapter one: Accessing, consuming, and creating information is increasingly decoupled from devices or single resources, and more personalized for the individual user. The forward-looking designer will learn about these technologies and how to leverage them for new and innovative user experiences.

With evolving technology and emerging markets around the globe, providing ubiquitous access to information is a major challenge. Devices are different, languages change, necessitating translations, devices are different, and GenAI needs to account for cultural differences. On a practical level, this can mean the requirement to have design teams or experts in different regions of the world. As discussed in Chap. 8 distributing teams can lead to challenges with design, consistency, and communication.

10.3.4 Content Representation

Content representation traditionally focuses on designing content organization systems based on semantic relationships of terms and concepts. Social networks, linked data from different sources, and content semantics are often intertwined to challenge the design skills of information architects. Many unsolved problems related to content representation, such as automatic metadata generation, controlled vocabularies and user's tagging integration, and using semantic networks for access and navigation, are very difficult challenges both for research and for implementations.

Despite these challenges people's desire for more and more content is almost insatiable. Improvements in metadata and cloud technology, and others, help us organize and deliver content to meet this growing need.

10.3.5 Digital Preservation

What happens to all this new information being created and stored (and can be deleted without a trace)? How can we track changes to dynamic websites (assuming we should) and AI generated content? How can users maintain different versions of documents on their device and cloud? Should information architects be responsible for these challenges? The answer is it depends on the preservation need, but IAs should certainly have an influence on any preservation effort.

As information comes and goes, people may not have access to the digital content previously available. And, as more companies rely on the digital space for their business, preserving content and data over a longer period of time has become important. Some businesses even have what are called "data warehouses" that store all sorts of data and content. Digital preservation techniques are needed to maintain access, and in some cases to comply with legal or other regulations. IAs can support preservation through metadata and design.

10.3.6 Voice and Gesture

Voice interfaces like Apple's SIRI and Amazon Alexa have become mainstream. The always on microphone can pick up commands; by simply by saying "Hey Alexa" a user can begin interaction through a connected device. While this is still considered a specialized topic area, many of the core UX concepts and principles apply here.

Gesture input is characterized usually by a touch screen, where swipes and multi-finger actions perform different tasks. IAs must be aware of limitations like the lack of interactions like "onHover" in a touch environment. Devices with eye tracking or hand/body tracking are offering more and more features that use movement for commands. As these technologies develop we can expect to see them leveraged in new and innovative ways.

Virtual reality (VR) is one way in which we see Voice and gesture come together in a very advanced way. In VR the user typically wears a headset and uses hand controllers or just their hands to move and manipulate their environment. Well, somewhat mature this field seems to still have a long way to go and a bright future. It's frequently used for gaming and training opportunities, even for things like flight simulators. As the user moves their heads and hands the system adapts the view and perspective. This is a substantially different experience than the typical smart phone or desktop computer.

10.3.7 Inclusive Design

Inclusive design is a growing area of focus for IAs, UX designers and businesses in general. Following the human-centered mindset, it requires that designers ensure people are not excluded from their digital products, with the mindset that access to the web, mobile apps, and other digital products is an essential human right. In practice, inclusive design can sometimes mean longer development cycles tech along with practical and technical challenges. This increases the need for IAs to get buying and partnership from business stakeholders.

Despite these challenges, inclusive design offers many benefits. An often cited example is curb cuts for wheelchair users to cross intersections. While initially designed for accessibility, these curb cuts are also useful for people pushing strollers, bicyclists, and others. In a digital space features like auto complete, voice control, and high contrast display settings are available to increase inclusivity for certain populations and are widely used features across all users. This shows how inclusive design can have unexpected benefits for all.

Sometimes, it's just good business. Many regions have laws around accessibility and inclusivity, good design will minimize your legal risks. And, over 1 billion people around the world are estimated to have some sort of disability. Inclusive design is more than just accessibility, but these examples show the broad inpact of inclusive design concepts. Inclusive design can increase your audience, enhance your brand reputation, and help make your designs more flexible for your users.

10.3.8 Customer Experience and Business Goals

Customer experience is a field that follows a customer (user) across all the "touchpoints" in relation to an organization. Touchpoints can include things like websites, in-person/in-store, and calling a customer care line. An important concept is that of the "customer journey," which shows interactions along with motivations, emotions, and outcomes. Oftentimes customer journeys are the same or very similar to user journeys that we covered in chapter four. Customer journeys typically include awareness of the brand or company, experiences with advertising or marketing and the resulting expectations.

With the rising importance of digital systems and people's higher and higher usability expectations, IAs and UX designers have increasing responsibilities to manage the customer journey and account for online and offline touchpoints as part of the overall user experience.

Along with this comes expectations that UX improves business outcomes. It is no longer enough that designers make things look aesthetically pleasing or make customers happy. Today, businesses demand that UX designs contribute to measurable outcomes. Well, this additional responsibility may seem daunting to some designers. In fact, we see it as a very good development. By focusing on business outcomes, UX teams can get a seat at the table for strategy and funding helping to grow the field. Good IAs and UX designers today understand the business, implications of their work and form strong relationships with business stakeholders.

10.3.9 Integrating Systems and Spaces

Integrating systems as the world becomes more and more complex remains a challenge. Advances in cloud, computing and networking provide IA the opportunity to bring together resources in new and exciting ways. However, we must also be aware of the context of use to make sure that these information channels are useful and don't just contribute to information overload. This will require substantial collaboration, design thinking and systems thinking.

While well equipped with the methods, principles, and human-centered mindset, UX teams need to work with other stakeholders to address issues in large systems. While often focused on a single interface or digital product, the ever more connected world means that IAs and designer must focus more and more on systems thinking, while maintaining a grounding in human-centered design and design thinking.

Design thinking has long been a part of the user experienced domain. It has been a common place where the boundaries between business and design are blurred. Many UX designers take on the responsibility of managing design, thinking projects in their organization because they have the skills, like user research, that are needed to complete the project successfully.

Systems thinking, while having a longer history in the business world, is a relative newcomer to the user experience community. Several new publications, such as articles and books have been published recently, that link the core skills to systems thinking and systems mapping and systems mapping. It's a very sensible evolution. IA has long been focused on integrating information spaces and systems, and the design skills to draw maps that increase stakeholders understanding fits squarely in the UX designers tool kit.

10.3.10 Human Centered AI

If you've been paying attention to the past nine chapters, you've seen that Artificial Intelligence (AI) has become a major component of IA and UX design. The IA community is rising to the occasion—The 2024 IA conference has the theme "IA in the Age of AI:

Designing Intelligent Information Landscapes," and the Dublin Core 2024 conference, "Trust, Transformation, and Humanity" is centered on the intersection of AI and metadata. UX and human–computer interaction publications have literally thousands of papers and presentations on human-centered AI (HCAI) and explainable AI (XAI). Leaders in the UX field from both industry and academia have turned their considerable skills towards making sure UX has a role in development of powerful new AI applications. Generative AI promises unlimited possibilities to provide highly personalized, adaptive and accessible user experiences and also makes the design processes significantly more efficient. Universities like Stanford and UC Berkeley have started human-centered AI departments, with governments around the world are involved as well. And, top tech companies have entire teams focused on HCAI. While many more challenges are sure to arise, there is a large contingent of researchers and practitioners working to ensure AI works for humans.

10.3.11 Higher Stakes

The rapid rise of generative AI applications and spread of AI presents new challenges for designers. Many AI systems we see today are low-stakes—if a movie recommendation is wrong nobody is harmed. However, AI is moving into situations with higher stakes, where the consequences are severe:

> How do we design and develop AI systems that have the potential to dictate whether or not someone receives a mortgage for a home purchase, or where to send first responders during a rapidly spreading wildfire?. (Barmer et al., 2021, p. 3)

These new questions, and higher stakes, will demand increasing attention in the coming years. The academic and industry communities are focused on ensuring a human-centered future, putting the human user first, with UX design as an emphasis (Shneiderman, 2020). Designers should look to partner with data scientists, machine learning engineers, and others in the AI field, bringing the much-needed human-centered approaches to ensure AI works for all.

Ozmen Garibay et al. (2023a, 2023b) gives us Six Human-Centered Artificial Intelligence Grand Challenges, including Human-AI interaction and a Design and Evaluation Framework "as a call for action to conduct research and development in AI that accelerates the movement towards more fair, equitable and sustainable societies" (p. 394). Using these and the other frameworks and guidelines we've shared in earlier chapters gives user experience professionals a roadmap for effective collaborations to address GAI challenges, such as minimizing potential biases in AI models, increasing explainability and transparency, and protecting user privacy. Also there's a delicate balance to strike between leveraging GAI's capabilities and maintaining user control and trust (Persona,

2024). Clearly, IAs, UX designers, and everyone on user experience teams will be important parts of researching, designing, and integrating information spaces in the current Generative Generation.

10.4 IA, UX Design and Beyond

We expect IA and UX design to continue well into the future. Before we end this journey in the land of information architecture and UX, let us revisit our description of information architecture given in Chap. 1:

> Information architecture is about organizing and simplifying information for its intended users; designing, integrating and aggregating information spaces to create usable systems or interfaces; creating ways for people to find, understand, exchange and manage information; and, therefore, stay on top of information and make right decisions.

We hope that it becomes clearer now that the point we emphasize throughout the book is that IA and UX design is not just about UI design or backend metadata and content. Rather, it is about helping people make use of information and make information systems and spaces work for them. Given the power and importance of emerging AI technologies, and the increasing reliance on digital and connected services and products, the human-centered approach seems to be more critical ever. The ultimate goal is to integrate information spaces into places where users can have productive and fulfilling experiences, and where technology and information is fully utilized to support people's goals and extend their abilities.

References

Barmer, H., Dzombak, R., Gaston, M., Palat, V., Redner, F., Smith, C., & Smith, T. (2021). *Human-centered AI*. Carnegie Mellon University.

Chessum, K., Liu, H., & Frommholz, I. (2023). An extended study of search user interface design focused on hofstede's cultural dimensions. In A. Holzinger, H. P. da Silva, J. Vanderdonckt, & L. Constantine, (Eds.), *Computer-human interaction research and applications. Communications in computer and information science*, vol. 1882. Springer Nature. https://doi.org/10.1007/978-3-031-41962-1_7.

Digital Web Magazine. http://www.digital-web.com/articles/secrets_of_a_successful_international_website/.

Drexel University. (n.d.). *Master's in human-computer interaction and user experience*. https://drexel.edu/cci/academics/masters-programs/ms-in-information-human-computer-interaction-ux/.

Frandsen-Thorlacius, O., Hornbæk, K., Hertzum, M., & Clemmensen, T. (2009). Non-universal usability?: A survey of how usability is understood by Chinese and Danish users. In *Proceedings of the SIGCHI conference on human factors in computing systems* (pp. 41–50). https://doi.org/10.1145/1518701.1518708.

Hall, E. T., & Hall, M. R. (1989). *Understanding cultural differences*. Intercultural press.

Hofstede, G. (1984). *Culture's consequences: International differences in work-related values*. Sage.

Iler, H. (2007). *It's in the details: Seven secrets of a successful international website*.

International Telecommunication Union (ITU). (2023a). *Facts and figures 2023—Internet use*. https://www.itu.int/itu-d/reports/statistics/2023/10/10/ff23-internet-use.

International Telecommunication Union (ITU). (2023b). *Mobile phone ownership*. https://www.itu.int/itu-d/reports/statistics/2023/10/10/ff23-mobile-phone-ownership/.

Internet Society Foundation. (2024). *What are the most used languages on the Internet?* https://www.isocfoundation.org/2023/05/what-are-the-most-used-languages-on-the-internet/.

Marcus, A., & Gould, E. (2000). Crosscurrents: Cultural dimensions and global web user-interface design. *Proceedings 6th Conference on Human Factors and the Web, 7*(4), 32–46. https://doi.org/10.1145/345190.345238.

Morville, P. (2003). *International information architecture*. http://semanticstudios.com/international_information_architecture/.

Morville, P. (2005). *Ambient findability: What we find changes who we become*.

Ozmen Garibay, O., Winslow, B., Andolina, S., Antona, M., Bodenschatz, A., Coursaris, C., Falco, G., Fiore, S. M., Garibay, I., Grieman, K. and Havens, J. C., & Xu, W. (2023a). Six human-centered artificial intelligence grand challenges. *International Journal of Human–Computer Interaction, 39*(3), 391–437.

Ozmen Garibay, O., Winslow, B., Andolina, S., Antona, M., Bodenschatz, A., Coursaris, C., Falco, G., Fiore, S. M., Garibay, I., Grieman, K. and Havens, J. C., & Xu, W. (2023b). Six human-centered artificial intelligence grand challenges. *International Journal of Human–Computer Interaction, 39*(3), 391–437. https://doi.org/10.1080/10447318.2022.2153320.

Pew Research Center. (2024). *Internet, broadband fact sheet*. https://www.pewresearch.org/internet/fact-sheet/internet-broadband/#internet-use-over-time.

Persona, L. (2024). Beyond efficiency and budgets: How generative AI Is transforming UX. https://www.forbes.com/councils/forbestechcouncil/2024/02/05/beyond-efficiency-and-budgets-how-generative-ai-is-transforming-ux/.

Plocher, T., Rau, P. L. P., & Choong, Y. Y. (2021). Cross-cultural design. In G. Salvendy (Ed.), *Handbook of human factors and ergonomics* (4th edn, pp. 162–191). https://doi.org/10.1002/9781118131350.ch6.

Shneiderman, B. (2020). Human-centered artificial intelligence: Three fresh ideas. *AIS Transactions on Human-Computer Interaction, 12*(3), 109–124. https://doi.org/10.17705/1thci.00131.

Sun, H. (2001). Building a culturally-competent corporate web site: An exploratory study of cultural markers in multilingual web design. In *Proceedings of the 19th annual international conference on computer documentation* (pp. 95–102). https://doi.org/10.1145/501516.501536

W3 Techs. (2024). *Usage statistics of content languages for websites*. https://w3techs.com/technologies/overview/content_language.

World Bank Group. (2024). *Individuals using the internet (% of population)*. https://data.worldbank.org/indicator/IT.NET.USER.ZS.

Würtz, E. (2005). A cross-cultural analysis of websites from high-context cultures and low-context cultures. *Journal of Computer-Mediated Communication, 11*(1), 274–299. https://doi.org/10.1111/j.1083-6101.2006.tb00313.x